A Communicative Course in English

STUDENT'S BOOK 1

VICTORIA KIMBROUGH

MICHAEL PALMER

DONN BYRNE

ODYSSEY, Student's Book 1

Library of Congress Cataloging in Publication Data

Kimbrough, Victoria, 1943-
Odyssey, a communicative course in English.

Includes index.
1. English language—Text-books for foreign students.
I. Palmer, Michael, 1935- . II. Byrne, Donn, 1929-
III. Title.
PE1128.K47 1983 428.2'4 82-20837
ISBN 0-582-90705-5 (paperback)
ISBN 0-8013-0327-3 (case)

First printing 1983

11 12-DO-95949392

Sponsoring Editor: Joanne Dresner
Project Editor: Nancy Perry
Cover Illustration: Kimmerle Milnazik
Design: Gloria Moyer
Production Manager: Anne Musso
Permissions and Photo Research: Claire Sanderson Hernandez
Photo and Art Credits: See page 86.

Longman, 10 Bank Street, White Plains, N.Y. 10606

Distributed in the United Kingdom by Longman Group Ltd., Longman House, Burnt Mill, Harlow, Essex CM20 2JE England, and by associated companies, branches and representatives throughout the world.

CONSULTANTS

TRINIDAD BOUZAS ABASCAL
Language Coordinator
Colegio Tepeyac
Mexico, D.F.

HUGO ACOSTA
Director
Instituto Electrónico de Idiomas
Bogotá, Colombia

LESLIE ADAMS
District Bilingual Resource Teacher
El Monte Union High School District
El Monte, California

FRANCISCO GOMES DE MATOS
Professor of Linguistics
Universidade Federal de Pernambuco
Recife, Brazil

CURTIS W. HAYES
Professor of Linguistics and ESL
University of Texas
San Antonio, Texas

MONA SCHERAGA
Instructor of ESL
Passaic High School
Passaic, New Jersey

CONTENTS

7 THIS IS RIVERDALE / 38

Structures

There is/there are
Some/any
Preposition *near*
Plurals with *-es*
Questions with *how many*

Functions

Asking and saying where places are
Asking for and giving personal information

8 A TALENT SHOW / 44

Structure

Can (to express ability)

Functions

Asking and saying what people can do
Describing people

9 WHAT CAN YOU SEE? / 50

Structures

Can in questions with *how many, what*
Object pronouns *it, them*
Preposition *to*

Functions

Asking for and giving information
Saying where things are

10 WHAT ARE YOU DOING? / 56

Structures

Present progressive tense, 1st, 2nd and 3rd persons singular, 3rd person plural
Object pronouns after prepositions *me, you, him, her, us, them*
Prepositions *behind, in front of, next to, with*
Questions with *what*

Functions

Asking and saying what people are doing
Asking and saying what time it is
Beginning a phone conversation
Greeting people

11 THE OK CORRAL / 62

Structures

Present progressive tense, 3rd person plural
Questions with *when*

Functions

Asking and saying what people are doing
Asking for and giving personal information

12 CARNIVAL DAY / 68

Structures

Review

Functions

Describing people
Extending and refusing an invitation

INTRODUCTION

ODYSSEY is a six-book series in English as a second or foreign language. It is designed for secondary students in private or public schools and young adults in language institutes. The language of the course follows a structural syllabus and is always presented in context. In addition to providing a firm foundation in grammar, ODYSSEY teaches students the communication skills they need to function in an English-speaking environment.

KEY FEATURES

A Clear Methodology

ODYSSEY is clear and easy to use. Teachers can immediately see the grammatical or communicative purpose of each exercise. Little preparation is necessary since the activities are easy to set up and explain. They are arranged so that they provide a pedagogically sound progression as well as a great deal of variety to hold students' interest.

ODYSSEY has been designed to fulfill the needs of students in large classes. All the oral exercises can be practiced by having the class as a whole respond. For more variety, however, these exercises can be done as small group or pair work. In addition to giving individuals more time to talk, small group or pair work lets students interact with each other and practice the language on their own.

Real Communication

Communication involves more than a knowledge of grammar. Although students may learn grammatical forms, it cannot be assumed that they will know how to use them to communicate. For this reason, students using ODYSSEY learn how they can use each structure, often in combination with other structures, to say something worthwhile or to accomplish a task. They talk about their interests, express opinions, solve problems and exchange information about their daily lives.

Throughout ODYSSEY, students move from controlled practice to more open-ended expression in both oral communication and writing. At the beginning of each unit, there are question-and-answer exercises, substitution exercises and short dialogs. Then, communicative dialogs recycle language items and give students the opportunity to talk about their own situations. Finally, at the end of each unit, expansion activities such as games and puzzles move students toward freer oral expression.

Students practice writing in exercises that are often derived from oral material and reading texts. At first, students follow strictly controlled patterns in exercises such as fill-ins and sentence completions. They are then gradually guided to write sentences and paragraphs, notes and letters, based on structures previously practiced.

Structural Control

The grammatical items presented in ODYSSEY have been selected and graded according to structural clarity and usefulness. Items are presented in a carefully sequenced progression. Students learn the most frequently used forms of each structure in contexts that illustrate how the language is used. They learn grammatical forms not as isolated items but as building blocks that can serve their communicative needs in English.

Content-based Units

Every other unit of ODYSSEY is based on a subject area such as science and history. Topics of interest to teenagers and young adults give students an opportunity to explore ideas while building their language skills in English. Students may be familiar with some of the topics in their native language, bringing with them prior knowledge which will motivate them to communicate in the new language.

A Strong Reading Component

Reading can be a rich and motivating way for students to expand their knowledge of the language. For some students it may be the principal means by which they make use of what they have learned.

The beginning of the course focuses on getting students interested in and used to reading English.

Texts on a wide range of topics and in a variety of styles are presented in each unit. These texts are carefully controlled for structure and vocabulary, incorporating language that students have already learned and exposing them to a few new forms that they will learn in later units. However, students, like native speakers, can understand far more than they can produce and can often infer the meaning of a word or structure from context. Therefore, as the course progresses, new vocabulary and structures are introduced into the readings, challenging the students and teaching them to understand new language from context.

ORGANIZATION OF THE STUDENT'S BOOK

There are twelve units in the Student's Book, two of which are for review. Each unit can be taught in approximately six to eight classroom periods. The units are divided into the following sections:

Presentation Text/Dialog

Key language structures are presented in the topic-centered **Texts** or storyline **Dialogs** at the beginning of each unit. The language is carefully controlled, with ungraded material introduced for recognition only when the context requires it. The alternation of **Dialogs** with topic-centered **Texts** helps to ensure that both spoken and written forms of the language are presented. Each **Presentation Text** or **Dialog** is supported by full-color artwork.

Do You Understand?

This section usually has two or three exercises which provide a quick comprehension check of the **Presentation Text** or **Dialog**. In Book One students are not expected to produce complete sentences since, at this level, emphasis is on comprehension. In most cases the exercises can be completed by answering *yes* or *no*, *right* or *wrong*, or by answering with one or two words. Sometimes the students simply have to point to the pictures. The exercises are intended to be done orally with the whole class.

Grammar

A study box listing the main structures presented and practiced in the unit heads the **Grammar** section. The exercises which follow relate directly to the content and artwork of the **Presentation Text** or **Dialog**. They give the students simple oral practice with the principal structures and vocabulary found there. The most common exercise types are "Make true sentences" and "Ask and answer the questions." The students are expected to produce complete sentences.

Practice

Students continue working with the key structures of the unit, but the **Practice** section usually presents new vocabulary and a different context in which to use the language. Structures from previous units are often recycled and integrated with the new grammar of the unit.

Most of the exercises are communicative and can be done with the whole class, in small groups or in pairs. At least one exercise in the **Practice** section gives the students the opportunity to talk about their own situations, activities or opinions. There may also be a written exercise emphasizing grammar, vocabulary or word order.

Review

Three or four mini-dialogs in the **Review** section provide controlled oral practice and integrate the key structures of the unit. Pictures cue the substitutions to be made, and parallel dialogs can be formed by using the other pictures in the set. The dialogs can be practiced first by having the class as a whole respond and then by having students work in pairs. A complete set of additional dialogs is given on pages 74–75 of the Student's Book.

Reading

The **Reading** texts in ODYSSEY are designed to consolidate what the students have previously learned and to develop their reading skills. The introduction of new structural and vocabulary items requires students to guess or infer meaning from context. The exercises usually check for general comprehension of the passage rather than focus on details.

Listening

A **Listening** section focusing on general comprehension is included in every other unit. It relates both thematically and linguistically to the **Reading** section of the unit. The script for the **Listening** section is printed on page 76 of the Student's Book and can also be used for additional activities such as dictation or reading for review.

Small Talk

These oral activities, in the form of short, communicative dialogs, are similar to the exercises in the **Practice** section, but they are less controlled. The **Small Talk** section provides further practice with the structures and vocabulary of the unit, while encouraging the students to have personal conversations. New grammar is occasionally introduced in these activities and is summarized in a study box at the head of the section.

Writing

A variety of exercises guides **Writing** practice. The exercises in the early units are carefully controlled; as the course progresses, **Writing** practice becomes more open-ended. These exercises may be used in class or, with the necessary oral preparation, given as homework.

Just for Fun

Language games, puzzles, quizzes, riddles and poems are some of the student-centered activities of the **Just for Fun** section. They may be used at any stage of a unit, or where suitable, given as homework. These activities are intended to provide an enjoyable way for students to use the skills they have learned.

COURSE COMPONENTS

The following components accompany each Student's Book:

- a **Teacher's Manual,** made up of the Student's Book, with notes on each page on how to present and practice the material. Each unit begins with a summary of the structures, functions and vocabulary presented. Answers to exercises are also included.

- a **Workbook,** which provides written practice of the key structures, functions and vocabulary of each unit. A variety of exercises including games and puzzles is designed for individual work. The **Workbook** exercises can be done in class with the students working alone or in pairs, or they can be assigned as homework.

- two **Cassettes,** consisting of recordings of the **Presentation Texts** and **Dialogs,** the mini-dialogs in the **Review** section, the **Listening** texts, and the dialogs of the **Small Talk** sections.

1 WHAT IS THIS?

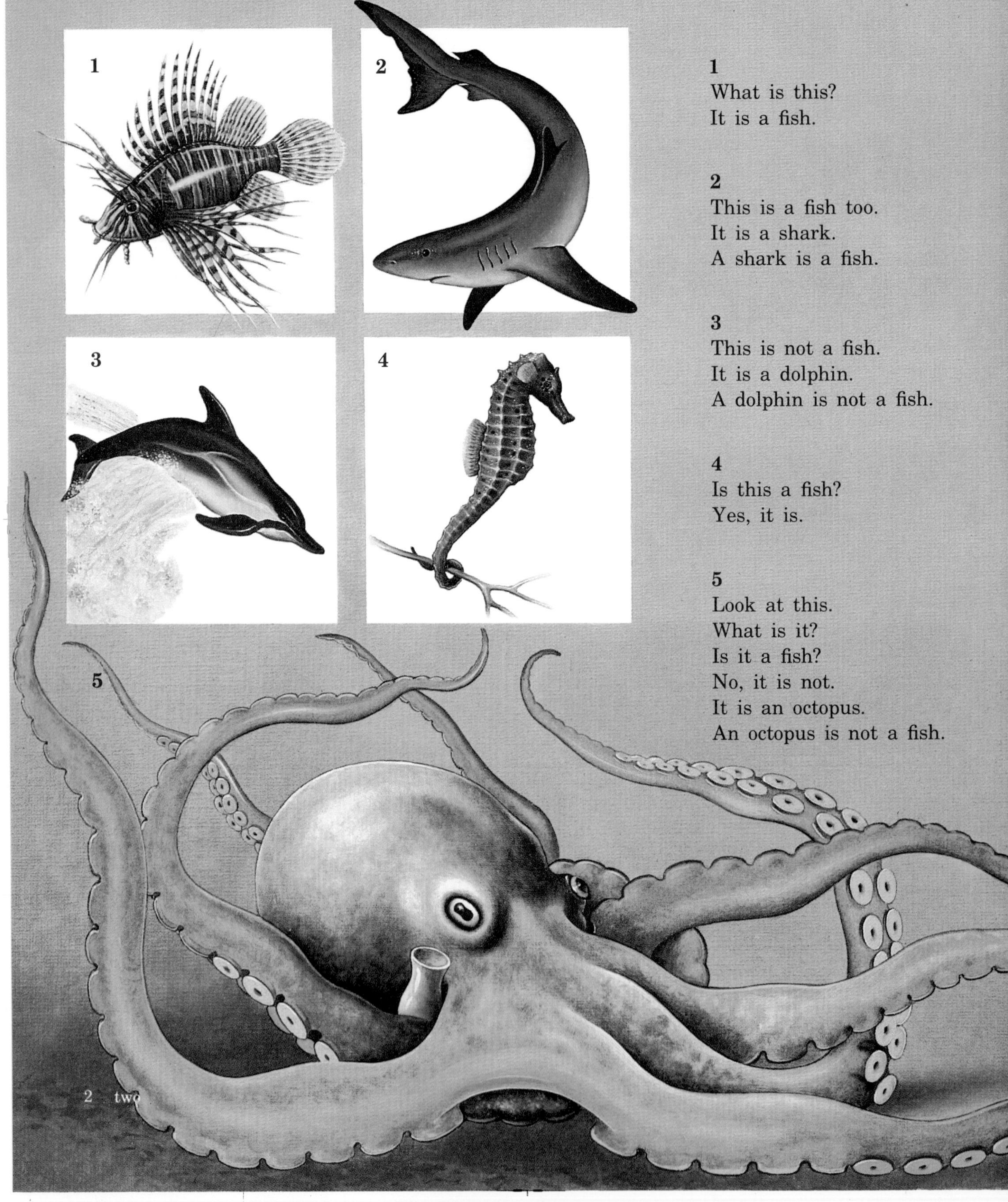

1
What is this?
It is a fish.

2
This is a fish too.
It is a shark.
A shark is a fish.

3
This is not a fish.
It is a dolphin.
A dolphin is not a fish.

4
Is this a fish?
Yes, it is.

5
Look at this.
What is it?
Is it a fish?
No, it is not.
It is an octopus.
An octopus is not a fish.

DO YOU UNDERSTAND?

1 Answer *yes* or *no*:

PICTURE ONE
Is this a fish?

PICTURE TWO
Is this a fish?

PICTURE THREE
Is this a fish?

PICTURE FOUR
Is this a dolphin?
Is it a fish?

PICTURE FIVE
Is this an octopus?
Is it a fish?

2 Right or wrong?

a. A shark is a fish.
b. A dolphin isn't a fish.
c. An octopus is a fish.

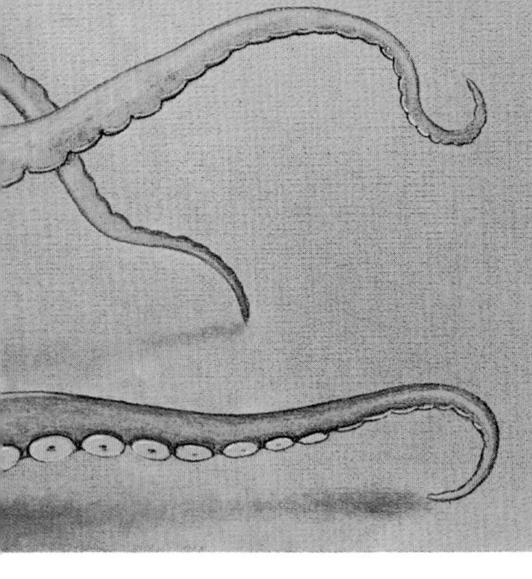

Grammar

<table>
<tr><td rowspan="2">This</td><td>is</td><td>a fish.</td></tr>
<tr><td>is not
isn't</td><td>an octopus.</td></tr>
</table>

<table>
<tr><td rowspan="2">Is</td><td rowspan="2">this</td><td rowspan="2">a fish?</td><td colspan="2">Yes, it is.</td></tr>
<tr><td>No, it</td><td>is not.
isn't.</td></tr>
<tr><td>What is
What's</td><td>this?</td><td></td><td>It is
It's</td><td>a fish.</td></tr>
</table>

**1 Point to the pictures.
Make true sentences:**

<table>
<tr><td>This</td><td>is
isn't</td><td>a fish.
a shark.
a dolphin.
an octopus.</td></tr>
</table>

**2 Point to the pictures.
Ask and answer the questions:**

a.
S1: What's this?
S2: It's *a dolphin/an octopus.*

b.
S1: Is this *a fish?*
S2: Yes, it is./No, it isn't.

1 Practice

1 Point to the pictures. Ask and answer the questions:

a.
S1: What's this?
S2: It's *a pen/an elephant.*

b.
S1: Is this *a bag*?
S2: No. This is *a bag.*

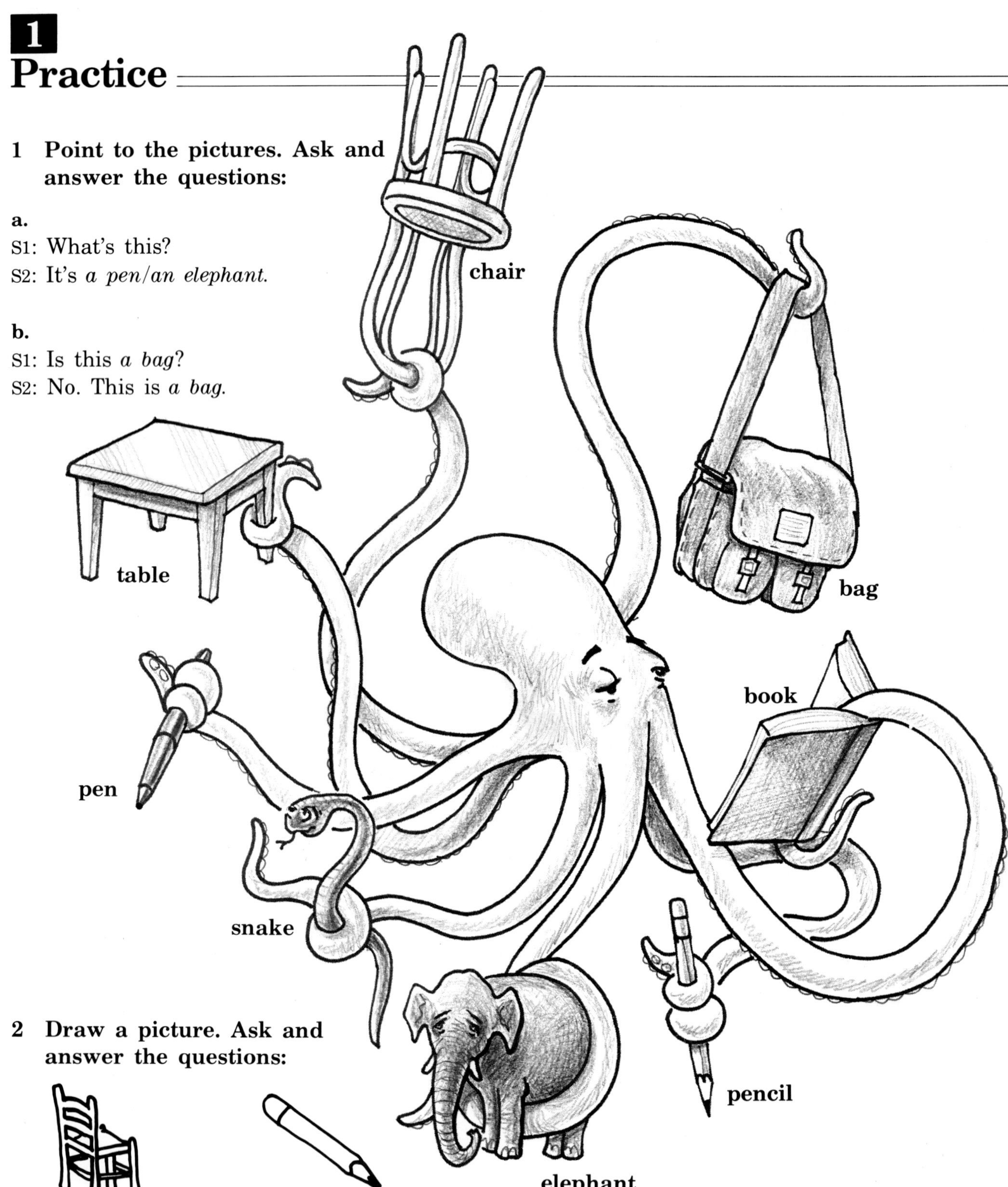

2 Draw a picture. Ask and answer the questions:

S1: What's this? **or** S1: What's this?
S2: Is it *a chair*? S2: Is it *a pen*?
S1: Yes. S1: No.
S2: Is it *a pencil*?
S1: Yes.

Review

3 Complete the conversation:

S1: What's this?
Is ......it...... a fish?
S2: No, ...
It's .... dolphin.

S1: And what's this?
S2: .... a fish.

Practice the conversations. Use different pictures.

1 octopus

2 snake

3 dolphin

4 fish

5 man

6 woman

1
S1: What's this?
S2: It's *an octopus.*

2
S1: Is this *an octopus*?
S2: Yes, it is.
S1: And what's this?
S2: It's *a dolphin.*

3
S1: Is this *a fish*?
S2: No, it isn't.
S1: What is it?
S2: It's *a snake.*

1

Reading

***A* describes Picture 1. Find the right picture for *B*, *C* and *D*.**

A
This is a fish.
It is a shark.
A shark is a fish.

B
This is not a fish.
It is not a snake.
It is a dolphin.
A dolphin is not a fish.

C
An octopus is an animal.
A snake is an animal too.
This is not an animal.
It is a guitar.

D
Look at this animal.
It is not an octopus.
It is an elephant.

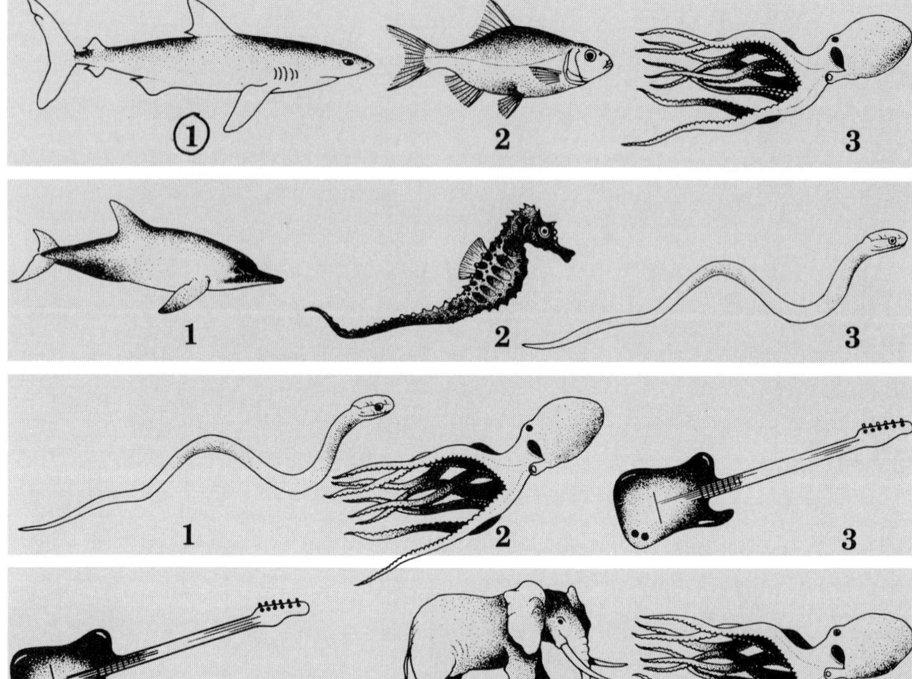

Listening

Point to the right picture above.

Small Talk

Here is	**my** book.
Here's	**your** book.

Practice the conversations:

1
S1: Here's your *book*.
S2: Thank you.

2
S1: Is this your *book*?
S2: Yes, it is. Thank you.
or
No, it isn't. This is my *book*.

Writing

1 Complete the conversation. Then practice it:

S1: Is this a *violin*?
S2: No, ...
S1: What .... it?
S2: .... *guitar*.
S1: .... it your *guitar*?
S2: Yes, ...

2 Practice more conversations. Use these words:

a. snake/fish
b. pen/pencil
c. chair/table

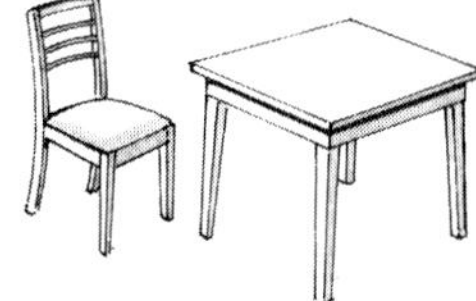

3 Choose pictures from page 6 and write sentences:

This is a shark.
A shark is a fish.

This is an octopus.
An octopus is not a fish.

Just for Fun

1 Find words in this box:

s	n	a	k	e	i	t	f	d	i
p	t	a	b	l	e	h	i	o	s
l	i	s	o	e	g	i	s	l	n
o	c	t	o	p	u	s	h	p	t
o	h	i	k	h	i	b	s	h	a
k	a	w	h	a	t	a	h	i	n
w	i	m	a	n	a	g	a	n	i
m	r	n	o	t	r	a	r	i	m
y	o	u	r	y	e	s	k	x	a
z	t	o	o	p	e	n	c	i	l

2 Write the words like this:

bag, a, is, snake, what . . .

3 Make sentences with the words:

This is a bag.
What is this?
A snake is not a fish.

4 Complete the words. Say the numbers and spell them:

1	2	3	4	5
one	t__o	__ __re__	fo__r	__i__e
6	**7**	**8**	**9**	**10**
si__	__e__en	__ __ght	ni__e	__en

2 WHAT'S YOUR

1
This is Jim.
He is a student.

2
This is Jim's sister.
She is a student too.
Her name is Debbie.

3
That is Tony.
He is an artist.
That is his car.

4

DEBBIE: Good morning. I like your picture.
TONY: Thank you.
DEBBIE: What's your name?
TONY: Tony Morales.
DEBBIE: My name is Debbie.
TONY: Hello, Debbie. Who's your friend?
DEBBIE: He isn't my friend. He's my brother. His name is Jim.

5

TONY: Hello, Tim.
JIM: My name isn't Tim. It's Jim.
TONY: Sorry, Jim.
DEBBIE: Is that your car over there?
TONY: Yes, it is.
DEBBIE: I like it.
JIM: What's that animal in your car?
DEBBIE: Is it a chimpanzee?
TONY: Yes. That's my friend, Ringo. Come and say hello.

NAME?

DO YOU UNDERSTAND?

1 Answer *yes* or *no*:

a. Is Jim a student?
b. Is Debbie a student?
c. Is Tony a student?
d. Is Ringo an artist?
e. Is Ringo a chimpanzee?

2 Say the names:

a. *He*'s an artist. (Tony)
b. *She*'s a student.
c. *She*'s Jim's sister.
d. *He*'s a student.
e. *He*'s Debbie's brother.
f. *His* chimpanzee's name is Ringo.

3 Right or wrong?

a. Debbie is a student.
b. Debbie is Tony's sister.
c. Jim is a chimpanzee.
d. Jim is Debbie's brother.
e. Tony is a student.

Grammar

Who is Who's		that?
That is That's		Jim.
He is **He's**		Debbie's brother.
He	is not isn't	an artist.
Is he		a student?
Yes, he is.		
What's **his** name?		

Who is Who's		that?
That is That's		Debbie.
She is **She's**		Jim's sister.
She	is not isn't	Jim's friend.
Is she		an artist?
No, she isn't.		
What's **her** name?		

1 Make true sentences:

Tony Debbie Jim Ringo	is isn't	a student. an artist. Jim's sister. Debbie's brother. a chimpanzee.

**2 Point to the pictures.
Ask and answer the questions:**

S1: Who's that?
S2: That's *Jim.*
S1: Is *he a student?*
S2: Yes, *he* is./No, *he* isn't.

3 Ask about your classmates:

S1: Who's that?
S2: That's *Isabel.*
S1: Is *she a student?*
S2: Yes, *she* is.

2 Practice

1 Point to the pictures.
Ask and answer the questions:

S1: What's *her* name?
S2: *Wonder Woman.*

1

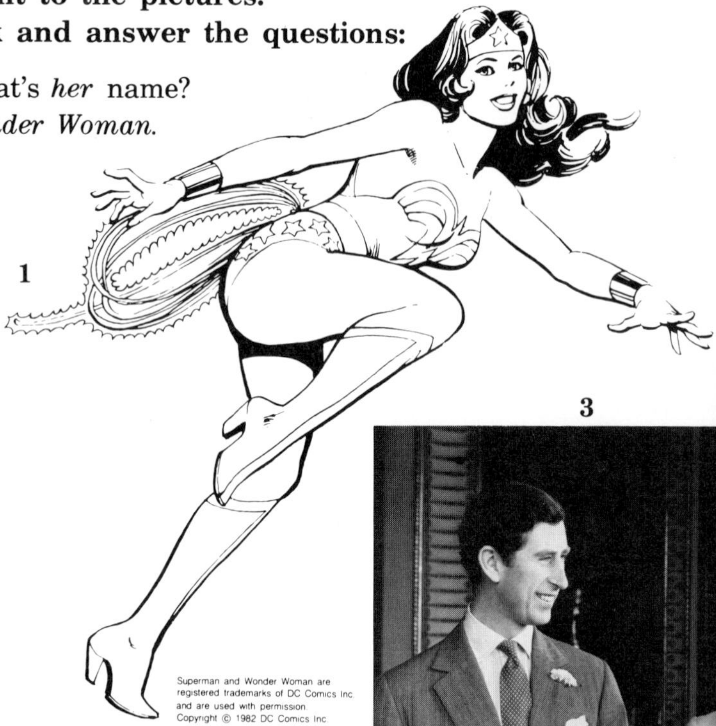

2

3

4

2 Ask about your classmates:

S1: What's *his* name?
S2: *David.*
S1: Is *he* a student?
S2: Yes.

3 This is Debbie's family:

father mother

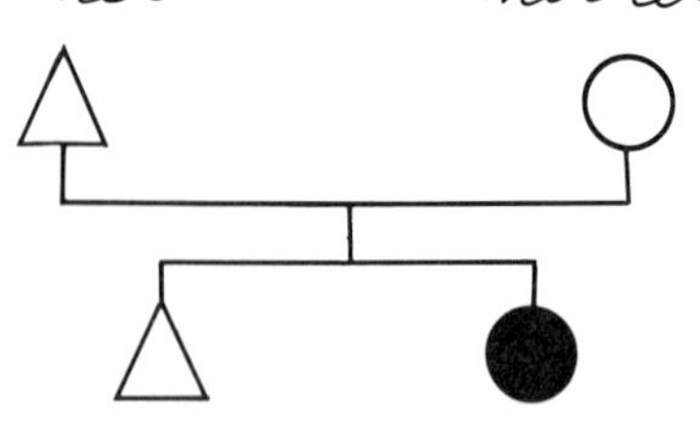

brother me

TONY: What's *his* name?
DEBBIE: *Jim.*
TONY: Is *he* a student?
DEBBIE: *Yes.*

Draw your family:

S1: What's *her* name?
S2: ....
S1: Is *she* a student?
S2: Yes./No. (*She*'s a ....)

5

6

1 Wonder Woman
2 Seiji Ozawa
3 Prince Charles, Queen Elizabeth, Princess Diana
4 Stevie Wonder
5 Jane Fonda
6 Superman

Review

Practice the conversations. Use different pictures.

1

S1: Who's that?
S2: That's *Jim. He*'s *a student.*
S1: Thanks.

2

S1: This is *Jim*'s *sister.*
S2: What's *her* name?
S1: *Debbie.*

3

S1: Is *Tony an artist?*
S2: Yes, *he* is.
S1: Is *his sister an artist* too?
S2: No, *she* isn't.

Jim	Debbie	Tony	Anita
a student	a student	an artist	a teacher
Debbie's brother	Jim's sister	Anita's brother	Tony's sister

2 Reading

Who is this?

This is Jim Marshall.
He is a student at Riverdale High School.
Riverdale is a city in California.
California is in the United States.
Jim is in the ninth (9th) grade.
His English teacher's name is Mr. Gordon.

This is Debbie Marshall.
She is Jim's sister.
She is at Riverdale High School too.
She is in the eleventh (11th) grade.
Her English teacher's name is Ms. Morales.

This is Tony Morales.
He is an artist.
That is his chimpanzee in the car.
The chimpanzee's name is Ringo.

This is Anita Morales.
She is Tony's sister.
She is a teacher at Riverdale High School.
She is Debbie's English teacher.
She is not at school now.
She is at home.

1 Right or wrong?

a. Riverdale is a city in California.
b. California is in the United States.
c. Jim is in the tenth grade.
d. Debbie is Jim's sister.
e. Debbie's teacher is Ms. Morales.
f. Anita's brother is a teacher too.
g. Mr. Gordon is an artist.
h. Tony is an artist.

2 Answer the questions:

a. Who's in Tony's car?
b. Who's in the ninth grade?
c. Who's Jim's sister?
d. Is Debbie at school now?
e. Is Anita at school now?

Small Talk

Practice the conversations:

1

S1: Hi! My name is *John.*
What's your name?
S2: *Joan.*
S1: I'm sorry. What's your name again?
S2: It's *Joan. J - O - A - N. Joan.*

2

S1: This is my friend, *Peter.*
Peter, this is *Joan.*
S2: Hello, *Peter.*
S3: Hi, *Joan.*

Writing

1 Write about yourself:

My name is ....
I am a student at .... School.
I am in the .... grade.
My English teacher's name is ....

2 Write about a friend:

This is my friend ....
He/She is .... student at ....
.... in the .... grade.
.... English teacher's name ....

Just for Fun

Ask about the people:

S1: *He's a movie star.*
What's *his* name?
S2: Is it *Charlie Chaplin?*
S1: Yes, it is.

Charlie Chaplin

Marie Curie
a scientist

Leonardo da Vinci
an artist

Shakespeare
a writer

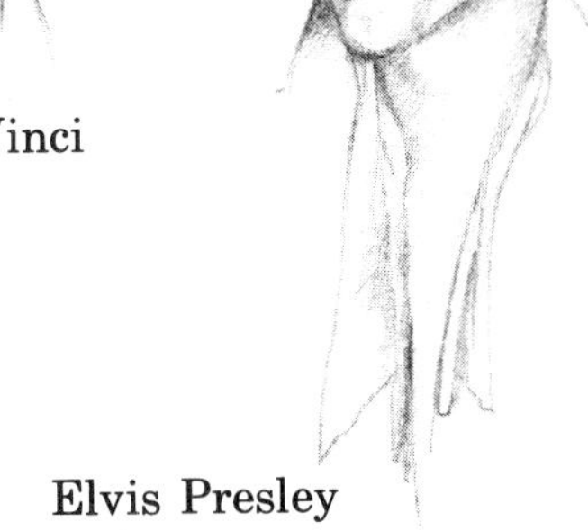

Elvis Presley
a singer

3 WHERE IS IT?

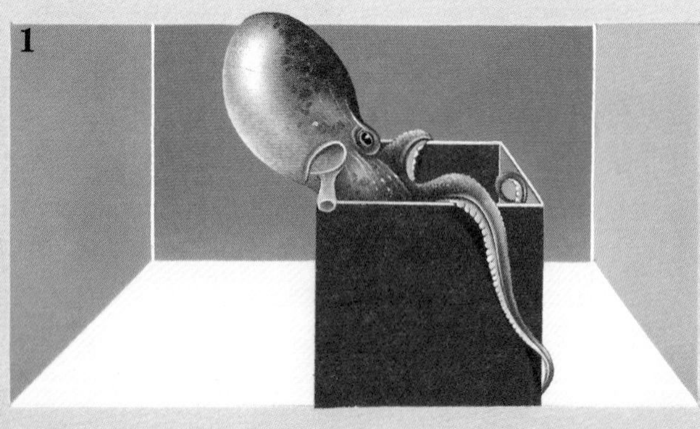

1
This is a picture of an octopus. The octopus is in a box. Which box? The red box. The box is red, and the octopus is red too.

2
In this picture the octopus is in a green box. It is the same octopus, but now it is green.

3
The octopus is not in the green box now. Where is it? It is under the white box. What color is the octopus in this picture? It is green and white.

4
Now the octopus is white, and the water is black.

DO YOU UNDERSTAND?

1 Right or wrong?

PICTURE ONE
The octopus is red.
It's in the box.

PICTURE TWO
The box is red.
The octopus is green.
It's in the box.
It's the same octopus.

PICTURE THREE
The octopus is in the box.
The octopus is green and white.

PICTURE FOUR
The octopus is in a box.
The octopus is black.
The water is black.

2 Answer the questions:

a. What color is the box in Picture One?
b. What color is the octopus in Picture One?
c. What color is the octopus in Picture Two?
d. What color is the box in Picture Three?
e. What color is the octopus in Picture Three?
f. What color is the water in Picture Four?

Grammar

The octopus is	green.	
It is It's	in under	the box.

What color is	the box?	It is It's	red.
Where is Where's	the octopus?	It is It's	in the box.

Which box?	The red box.

1 Point to the pictures and say:

a.

This is a [green / white / red] box.

b.

The octopus is [white. / red. / green. / green and white.]

2 Ask and answer the questions:

a.
S1: What color is the octopus in Picture *One*?
S2: It's *red*.

b.
S1: Where's the octopus in Picture *One*?

S2: It's [in / under] the [white / green / red] box.

3

Practice

1 Point to the pictures. Ask and answer the questions:

S1: What color is this *book?*
S2: It's *red.*

2 Ask and answer the questions:

S1: Where's the *box?*
S2: Which *box?*
S1: The *yellow box.*
S2: It's *on* the *table.*

The box is **on** the table.

3 Complete the note:

11/28

Mike,
I'm at home. I need my pen and my pencil. My book is blue. It's ___ my desk. My pencil is ___, and it's ___ my book. My pen is ___ my book. It's ___.

Thanks,
Gary

white

black

red

green

blue

yellow

Review

Practice the conversations. Use different pictures.

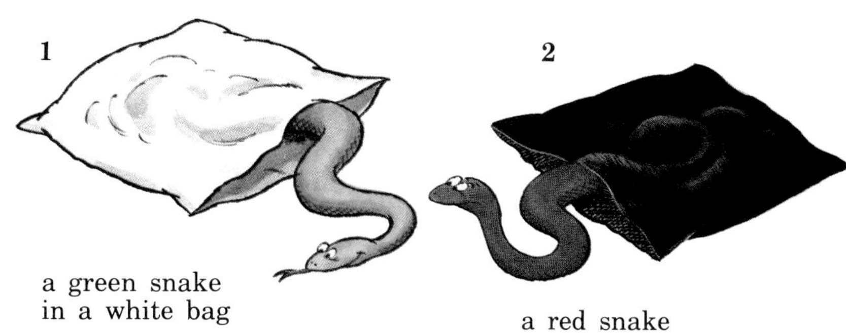

1 a green snake in a white bag

2 a red snake in a black bag

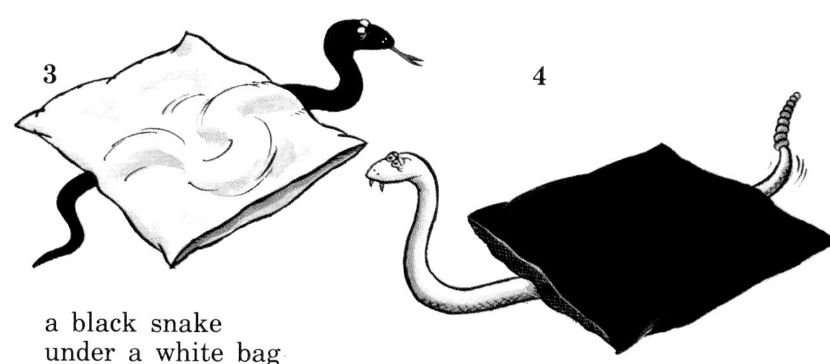

3 a black snake under a white bag

4 a white snake under a black bag

1

S1: Look! A snake!
S2: A snake? Where?
S1: *In* that bag.
S2: Which bag?
S1: The *black* bag.

2

S1: Is that a snake?
S2: Where?
S1: *Under* the *white* bag.
S2: Yes! Run!

3

S1: Hey! What's that?
S2: It's a snake.
S1: Really?
S2: Yes. It's a *red* snake.

3 Reading

Read about Jim's trick:

Where is the key?

In Picture Two the key is not really *in* the glass. It is *under* the glass.

Look at Picture Three again. The key is in Jim's hand. His hand is in his pocket.

1 Point to:

a glass of water	a key
a hand	a pocket
a glass on a table	a black bag

2 Answer the questions:

a. Is the key really in the glass in Picture Two?
b. Where is the key in Picture Three?

Listening

Answer the questions:

Where is the key in Picture Four?
Is it in the bag?
Is it under the table?
Is it in Jim's pocket?

Small Talk

Practice with a classmate:

S1: Here's your *pen.*
S2: Thank you.
or
S1: Here's your *pencil.*
S2: That isn't my *pencil.*
My *pencil* is *blue.*
S1: Oh, sorry.

Writing

Read about Rob's hat:

Rob's *hat* is not *under the table.*
It is not *on the chair.*
It is not *in Rob's bag.*
It is *in his pocket!*

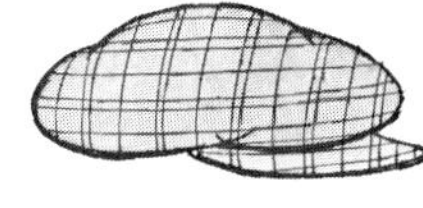

Now write about Rob's pen, his book and his bag.

Just for Fun

1 Ask and answer the questions:

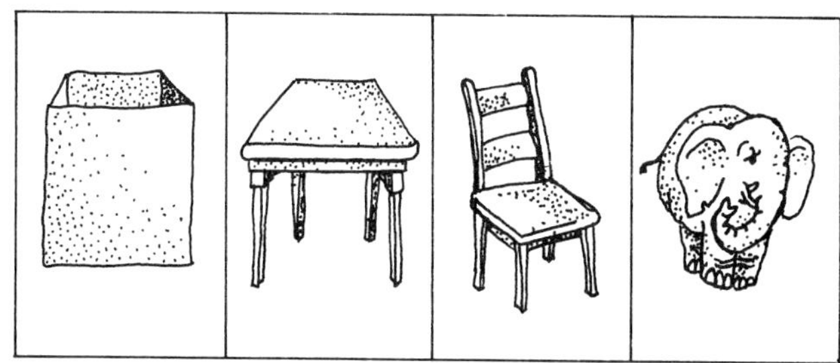

a.
S1: What's this?
S2: It's *a box.*

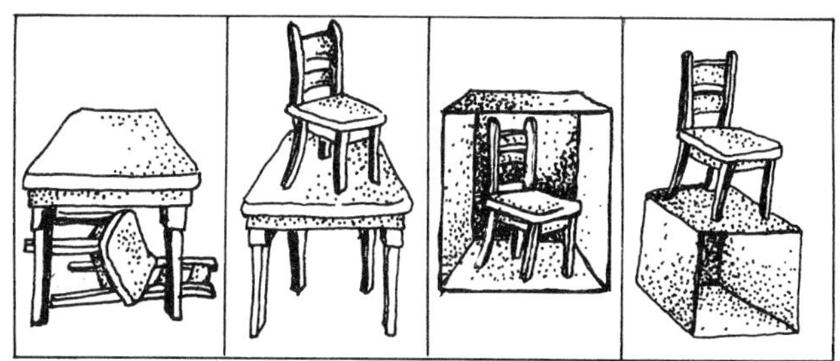

b.
S1: Where's the chair?
S2: It's *under* the *table.*

2 Ask and answer questions about these pictures:

3 Write the numbers and say them:

10 11 .... 14 ....
16 17 .... 19 ....

4 WHERE ARE YOU

1

Today is Saturday. Jim and Debbie are not at school. They are in Riverdale Park. Tony is there too.

2

DEBBIE: Hello, Tony. How are you today?
TONY: I'm fine, thanks. How are you?
DEBBIE: Fine, thanks.
JIM: You're really a good singer, Tony. I like that song!
DEBBIE: I like it too. It's very good.
JIM: It's great!
TONY: Thanks. It's not bad.

3

DEBBIE: Look at that bus.
JIM: Oh! Who are those girls?
DEBBIE: I don't know. They aren't from Riverdale. Where are they from?
TONY: They're from Canada.
DEBBIE: Are they students?
TONY: Yes. They're art students. Hi, Anne. Hi, Mary.

4

MARY: Hi, Tony!
ANNE: Hi, Tony! Is that your chimpanzee?
TONY: Yes.
MARY: What's his name?
TONY: Ringo.
MARY: Hello, Ringo. How are you?

FROM?

DO YOU UNDERSTAND?

1 Right or wrong?

a. Tony is in Riverdale Park.
b. Jim and Debbie like Tony's song.
c. The girls in the bus are from Riverdale.
d. Anne and Mary are art students.
e. Tony is Ringo's chimpanzee.

2 Say the names:

a. *They* like Tony's song.
b. *He*'s a good singer.
c. *They*'re from Canada.
d. *They*'re students, and *they*'re from Riverdale.
e. Ringo is *his* chimpanzee.

3 Which is right?

It's great! =

a. I'm fine.
b. It's very good.
c. It's bad.

Hi! =

a. Goodbye.
b. Thanks.
c. Hello.

Grammar

Those girls are	students.
They are **They're**	art students.
They are not They aren't	from Riverdale.

Are they	in Riverdale? at school? from Riverdale?	Yes, they are. No, they aren't.
Where are they from?		They're from Canada.

1 Answer the questions:

a. Is Tony in Riverdale Park?
b. Are Jim and Debbie at school?
c. Is Tony a good singer?
d. Are Anne and Mary from the United States?
e. Are they friends?

2 Ask and answer the questions:

a.

S1: Are	Jim and Debbie Anne and Mary	students friends from Canada from Riverdale	?

S2: Yes, they are./No, they aren't.

b.

S1: Where are *Anne and Mary* from?
S2: *Canada.*
S1: Are they *students?*
S2: Yes, they are./No, they aren't.

4

Practice

1 Point to the pictures and say:

He's a *teacher.*
She's a *dancer.*
They're *singers.*

2 Point to the pictures.
Ask and answer the questions:

a.
S1: Is *he* a good *teacher?*
S2: Yes, *he* is./No, *he* isn't.

b.
S1: Are they good *singers?*
S2: Yes, they are./No, they aren't.

a student

a teacher

a guitarist

dancers

3 Complete the conversation:

S1: *Are* .... they from the United States?
S2: No, they ....
S1: Where .... they .... ?
S2: I think they're .... Spain.
S1: Oh. .... students?
S2: No, ... dancers.

students

singers

4 Write the day and say it:

Mon. *Monday*
Tues. ....
Wed. ....
Thurs. ....
Fri. ....
Sat. ....
Sun. ....

5 Ask and answer the question:

S1: What day is today?
S2: It's *Wednesday.*

4

Review

Practice the conversations. Use different pictures.

1

S1: Who are those *girls?*
S2: They're *singers.* They're from *the United States.*

2

S1: Where are those *boys* from?
S2: *Greece.*
S1: They're good *singers!*

3

S1: Are those *girls* from *Brazil?*
S2: Yes, they are.
S1: Are they *singers?*
S2: No, they aren't. They're *guitarists.*

4 Reading

Who is your favorite rock star?

My favorite rock star is Paul McCartney. He is a good singer and a good guitarist. He is a very good song writer too. His song "Yesterday" is my favorite song.

Here is a picture of Paul and a rock group. His wife is in this group. Her name is Linda, and she is American. She is a singer too.

The guitarists are English. Their names are Denny and Laurence, and they are very good.

The drummer, Steve, is from England too. He is a great drummer!

1 Point to:

a. a rock group
b. an American singer
c. a song writer
d. three guitarists
e. Mrs. McCartney
f. a drummer

2 Say the names:

a. *She*'s a singer.
b. *They*'re from England.
c. *She*'s Paul's wife.
d. *He*'s a drummer.
e. *He*'s a song writer.
f. *They*'re good guitarists.

Small Talk

You are You're	a good singer.	
Are you	a good student?	Yes, **I** am. No, **I'm** not.

Practice the conversations:

1

S1: Are you a good *singer?*
S2: Yes, I am./No, I'm not.
What about you?
S1: I'm not very good./I'm not bad.

2

S1: Hello, I'm *Annette.*
S2: Hi, I'm *Paul.*
S1: Where are you from?
S2: *The United States.* What about you?
S1: I'm from *Canada.*

Writing

1 Make words with "er" or "ist":

sing
teach + er

art
guitar + ist

2 Complete the sentences:

a. Anita Morales is a teacher.
b. Paul McCartney is a ....
c. He is a .... too.
d. Tony Morales is an ....

3 Write about a singer:

I like .... He/She is a .... singer. .... from .... songs .... very good.

Just for Fun

**1 Draw an elephant. Hide it.
Ask and answer the questions:**

S1: Where's your elephant?
Is it *under that bag?*
S2: No, it isn't.
S1: Is it *in your pocket?*
S2: Yes, it is.

**2 Draw some snakes. Hide them.
Ask and answer the questions:**

S1: Where are your snakes?
Are they *on that table?*
S2: No, they aren't.

5 THAT'S LIFE

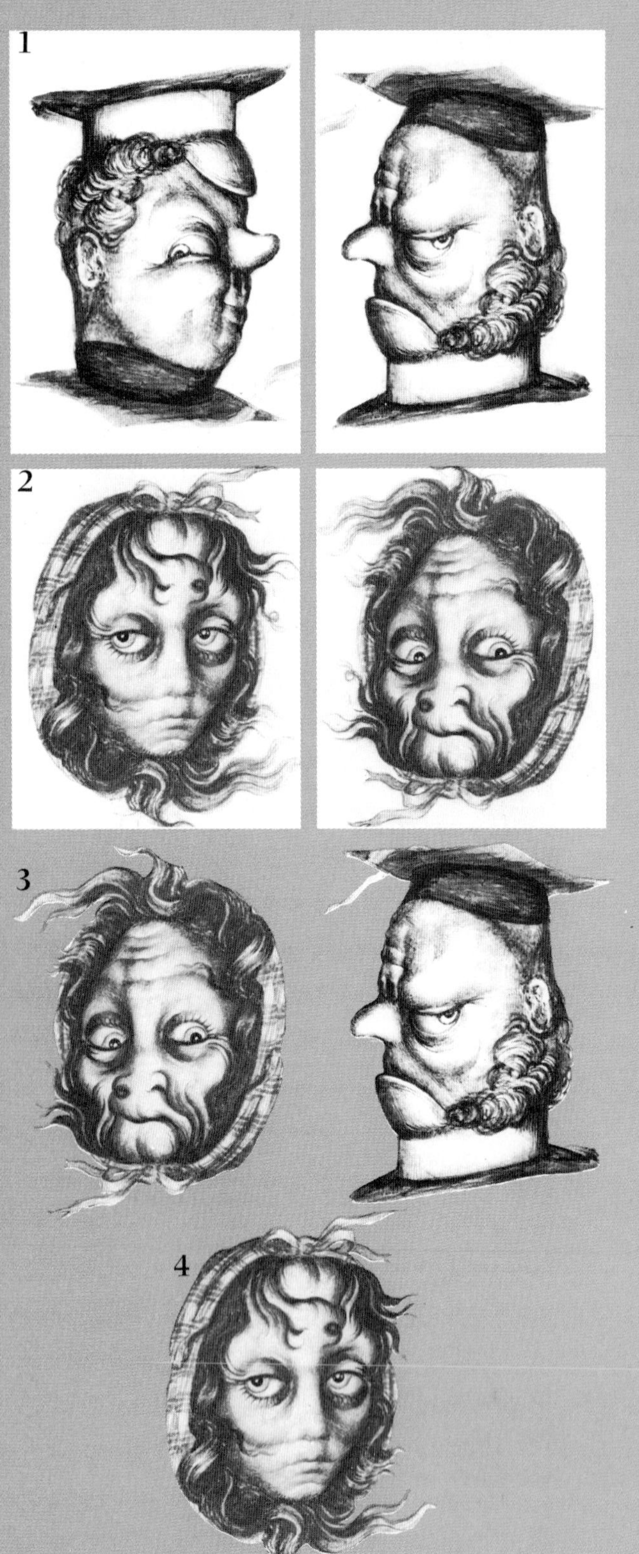

1

Look at these men. They are English. Their names are Mr. Black and Mr. White. Mr. Black is twenty years old. He is young and happy. Mr. White is an old man. He is not happy.

2

Look at these women. They are American. Their names are Miss Green and Mrs. Brown. Miss Green is young, and Mrs. Brown is old. They are sad. But look at these women again.

Look at the pictures like this. Now Miss Green is old, and Mrs. Brown is young.

These pictures are really the same. Maybe Miss Green and Mrs. Brown are really the same woman.

3

Listen to Mr. White:
"Sometimes we're happy, but sometimes we aren't happy. That's life."

4

Listen to Miss Green:
"I'm young. Sometimes I'm happy, but now I'm sad. That's life. Sometimes you're happy, sometimes you're sad."

DO YOU UNDERSTAND?

1 Right or wrong?

a. Mr. White and Mr. Black are American.
b. Mr. Black is old.
c. Mr. White is happy.
d. Miss Green is young.
e. Mrs. Brown is old.
f. Miss Green and Mrs. Brown are sad.

2 Say the names:

a. *They*'re English.
b. *They*'re young.
c. *She*'s old.
d. *She*'s young.
e. *They* aren't happy.
f. *He* isn't sad.

3 Answer the questions:

a. Who's young?
b. Who's old?
c. Who's happy?
d. Who's sad?

Grammar

Look at	**these**	**men.** **women.**

Their names are	Mr. White and Mr. Black. Miss Green and Mrs. Brown.	
They are They're	English. American.	
Are they	sad? happy?	Yes, they are. No, they aren't.

1 Point to the pictures.
Ask and answer the questions:

S1: What's *her* name?
S2: *Miss Green.*
S1: What are their names?
S2: *Mr. Black* and *Mr. White.*

2 Point to the pictures.
Make true sentences:

This	man woman	is	American. English. young. old. sad. happy.
These	men women	are	

3 Ask and answer the questions:

a.
S1: Is *Miss Green young?*
S2: Yes, *she* is./No, *she* isn't.

b.
S1: Are *Mr. Black* and *Mr. White American?*
S2: Yes, they are./No, they aren't.

5 Practice

1 Dusty Baker
U.S.—baseball player

2 Fernando Valenzuela
Mexico—baseball player

3 Giorgio Chinaglia
Italy—soccer player

4 Franz Beckenbauer
Germany—soccer player

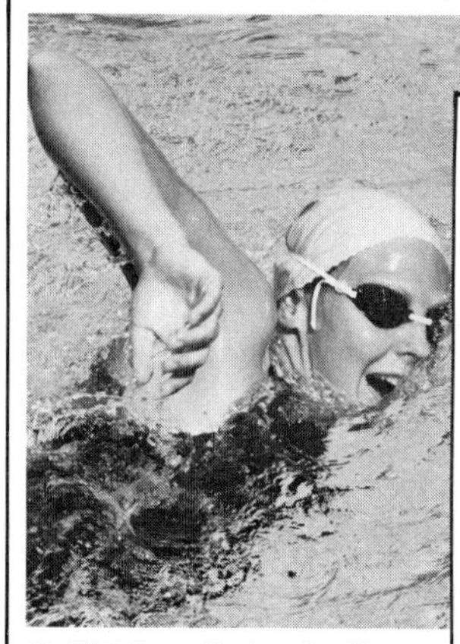
5 Shirley Babashoff
U.S.—swimmer

6 Shigehiro Takahashi
Japan—swimmer

1 Point to the pictures and say:

S1: These *men* are *football players.*
S2: This *woman* is a *swimmer.*

2 Who is it?

a.

S1: *She*'s a *tennis player.*
She's from *the United States.*
What's *her* name?
S2: *Tracy Austin.*

b.

S1: They're *football players.*
They're from *The United States* and *England.*
What are their names?
S2: *Richard Todd* and *John Smith.*

7 Tracy Austin
U.S.—tennis player

8 Hana Mandlikova
Czechoslovakia—
tennis player

9 Richard Todd
U.S.—football player

10 John Smith
England—football player

3 Ask your classmates:

S1: What's your favorite sport, *David?*
S2: *Soccer.*
S1: What's your favorite sport, *Sara?*
S2: *Soccer.*

Use this form:

football	
soccer	✓ ✓
tennis	
swimming	
baseball	

5

Review

Practice the conversations. Use different pictures.

1

S1: Hey! Look at the *football players.* What are their names?
S2: *Paul* and *Tom.*
S1: Are they English or American?
S2: *American.*

2

S1: Look! *Pat* and *Mandy!*
S2: Who are they?
S1: They're *American swimmers.*
S2: They're great!

3

S1: *Kay* and *June* are great *tennis players!*
S2: Where are they from?
S1: They're from *England.*

1 Paul and Tom American football players

2 Pat and Mandy American swimmers

3 Kay and June English tennis players

4 Bill and Andy English gymnasts

5 Reading

How old are they?

Look at the numbers in the squares:

One		
(4) 5	6	7
12	13	14
15		20

Two		
(2) 3	6	7
10	11	14
15	18	19

Three		
(1) 3	5	7
9	11	13
15	17	19

Four		
(8)	9	10
11	12	13
14		15

Five		
(16)	17	18
19		20

Debbie is seventeen years old. Where is the number seventeen? It is in Squares Three and Five.

Add up the first numbers in those squares. The numbers are one and sixteen. The answer is seventeen. That is Debbie's age.

Jim's age is in Squares One, Two and Four. How old is he?

Listening

Answer the question:

John and Mike are Debbie's friends.
How old are they?

Small Talk

How old are you?
I'm thirteen years **old.**

Practice the conversations:

1

S1: How old are you?
S2: I'm *thirteen* years old.
How old are you?
S1: I'm *thirteen too.*
S2: How old is *Kim?*
S1: She's *fourteen.*

2

S1: I'm good at *English.*
What about you?
S2: I'm not very good at *English,*
but I'm good at *music.*

Writing

Read about Jim:

2204 Vista Drive
Riverdale, California 95032
February 16, 1984

Dear Pen Pal,

My name is Jim Marshall, and I am a student at Riverdale High School in Riverdale, California. I am fourteen years old, and I am in the ninth grade.

I am very good at sports and music, but I am not very good at math. What about you? What are you good at?

1 Talk and write about Jim's friend Isabel:

Isabel is like Jim. She is fourteen years old. She is a student at . . .

2 Talk and write about Jim and Isabel:

Jim and Isabel are fourteen years old. They are students at . . .

3 What about you?
Talk and write about yourself.

Just For Fun

We are **We're**	students.	
Are you	actors? English?	Yes, **we are.** No, **we aren't.**

Guess the occupation and nationality of your classmates:

S1: Are you *actors*?
S2 & S3: Yes, we are.
S1: Are you *English*?
S2 & S3: No, we aren't.
S1: . . .

6 WHERE'S RINGO?

1

TONY: Where's Ringo?
DEBBIE: I don't know. Ask that policeman.

2

TONY: Excuse me. Can you help me, please?
POLICEMAN: What's the problem?
TONY: It's Ringo.
POLICEMAN: Ringo? Who's Ringo?
TONY: He's my chimpanzee.
POLICEMAN: Really? And who are you? Are you from a circus?
TONY: No. I'm an artist. My name is Tony Morales.
POLICEMAN: I see. Now, what about the chimpanzee? Where is it?
TONY: I don't know. That's the problem.

3

JIM: Look! There's Ringo!
TONY: Come here, Ringo!
POLICEMAN: Is that your chimpanzee?
TONY: Yes. That's Ringo.

4

POLICEMAN: Who are those girls?
DEBBIE: They're our friends. They're Canadian.
ANNE: We're from Montreal.
POLICEMAN: I see. And whose bus is that?
MARY: It's our bus.
TONY: Thanks for your help.
POLICEMAN: You're welcome.
DEBBIE: Thanks again. Goodbye.

DO YOU UNDERSTAND?

1 Right or wrong?

a. Ringo isn't in Tony's car.
b. Ringo is from a circus.
c. Anne and Mary are Debbie's friends.
d. They're from California.

2 Point to the pictures and say:

a. He's an artist.
b. He's Tony's chimpanzee.
c. He's a policeman.
d. She's American.
e. They're Canadian.

Grammar

1 Ask and answer the questions:

a.

S1: Is *Tony*	an artist in Riverdale Park a student from California from Montreal	?

S2: Yes, *he* is./No, *he* isn't.

b.

S1: Are	Jim and Debbie Anne and Mary	Tony's friends in the bus friends from Canada	?

S2: Yes, they are./No, they aren't.

c.

S1: Where is *Tony* from?
S2: *California.*
S1: What city is *he* from?
S2: *Riverdale.*

Whose car is that?
It's Tony**'s.**

2 Point to the pictures. Ask and answer the questions:

S1: Whose	bus hat car chimpanzee	is that?

S2: It's	Tony's. the policeman's. Anne and Mary's.

6

Practice

1 Point to the pictures. Ask and answer the questions:

a.

S1: What's *this?*
S2: It's *an elephant.*
S1: Whose *elephant* is it?
S2: It's *his elephant.*

b.

S1: What are *those?*
S2: They're *horses.*
S1: Whose *horses* are they?
S2: They're *her horses.*

2 Ask and answer the questions:

a.

S1: Where's the *snake?*
S2: It's *under* the *black box.*

b.

S1: Where are the *lions?*
S2: They're *on* the *yellow box.*

3 Ask your classmates:

a.

S1: Excuse me. Is this your *pen?*
S2: Yes, it is. Thank you.
S1: You're welcome.

or

S1: Excuse me. Is this your *book?*
S2: No, it isn't. My *book* is *blue.*/
My *book* is *on my desk.*

b.

S1: Whose *book* is this?
S2: It's *Yoko*'s.

4 **Complete the conversation:**

S1: Are these your keys?
S2: No, ...they.... aren't.
Here are .... keys.
S1: .... they Jill's keys?
S2: No. .... keys are in the car. Maybe they're Sam's keys.
S1: No. .... keys are over there.
S2: Are they Anne and Mary's keys?
S1: Maybe. I think .... keys are green too.

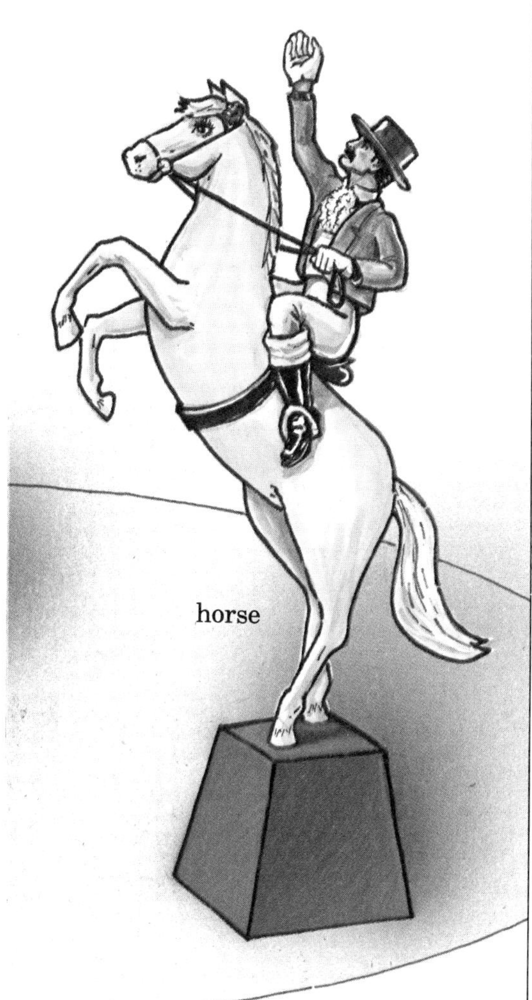

Review

Practice the conversations. Use different pictures.

1

S1: Whose car is that?
S2: Which car?
S1: The *green* car.
S2: It's *Tony*'s.

2

S1: Is that your car?
S2: Which car?
S1: The *black* car.
S2: No, my car is *yellow*. That's *Tom*'s car.

3

S1: Is that *Tony*'s car?
S2: Which car?
S1: The *red* car.
S2: No, that's *Linda*'s.

4

S1: Who's that *woman* in the *white* car?
S2: That's *Kathy.*
S1: Is *she American?*
S2: No. *She*'s *English.*
S1: What city is *she* from?
S2: I don't know.

6 Reading

A letter to a rock star

Who is it to?
Who is it from?

Rua Rocha, 74
Rio de Janeiro
March 3, 1984

Dear Paul,
My name is Carlos da Costa. I am Brazilian. I am thirteen years old, and I am a student at Bela Vista School in Rio de Janeiro.
I like your music very much. You are a very good song writer. You are my favorite singer.
Here is a picture of you. Please write your name on it, and send it to me. Please write a letter to me too.
Thank you very much.

Sincerely,
Carlos da Costa

1 Point to:

a. Carlos da Costa's address
b. the name of a Brazilian student
c. the name of his school
d. a picture of his favorite singer

2 Answer the questions:

a. Who's this letter to?
b. Who's it from?
c. What's his address?
d. How old is he?
e. What nationality is he?
f. What city is he from?
g. Who's his favorite singer?

3 Complete the sentences:

a. My *name* is Carlos da Costa.
b. You are my favorite ....
c. Here is a .... of you.
d. Please write your .... on it.
e. Please write a .... to me.

Small Talk

Practice the conversation. Then talk to a classmate:

S1: Hi, I'm *Rosa.*
S2: Hello, my name is *Carlos.*
S1: Where are you from, *Carlos?*
S2: *Brazil.* What about you?
S1: I'm from *Mexico.*
S2: What city are you from?
S1: *Mexico City.* What about you?
S2: I'm from *Rio de Janeiro.*
S1: Are you a student?
S2: Yes. Are you a student too?
S1: Yes, I am.

Writing

Look at these cards:

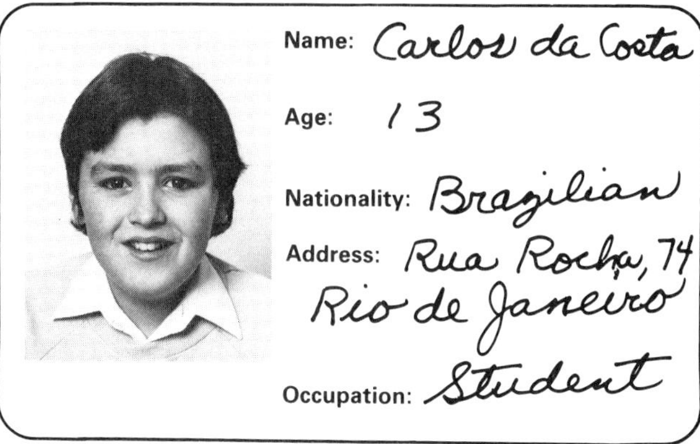
Name: Carlos da Costa
Age: 13
Nationality: Brazilian
Address: Rua Rocha, 74
Rio de Janeiro
Occupation: Student

Name: Anne Kaplan
Age: 21
Nationality American
Address: 18 West 70 Street
New York, NY 10023
Occupation Art Student

Carlos da Costa is a student. He is thirteen years old, and he is Brazilian. He is from Rio de Janeiro.

1 **Write about Anne Kaplan.**

2 **Write about yourself.**

Just for Fun

1 **Can you say these sentences quickly?**

Whose hat is that?
That's Harry's hat.
This is Harry.
That's his hat.

2 **What are the next numbers?**

a. 10, 20, 30, 40
b. 4, 8, 12, 16, ...
c. 21, 32, 43, ...
d. 1, 2, 4, 7, 11, ...

3 **Find the words and make sentences:**

Y	H	T	B	Z	H	H	T	D	G
B	F	N	N	A	M	E	H	S	K
R	X	A	Y	F	C	E	E	I	S
C	O	J	C	G	C	R	I	N	R
X	J	P	D	W	A	C	N	G	F
Z	F	A	V	O	R	I	T	E	J
C	I	U	Q	F	T	K	D	R	C
N	U	L	E	Q	N	T	G	L	I
U	X	P	O	O	E	V	Y	T	S
S	D	L	E	M	Y	B	H	P	A

7 THIS IS RIVERDALE

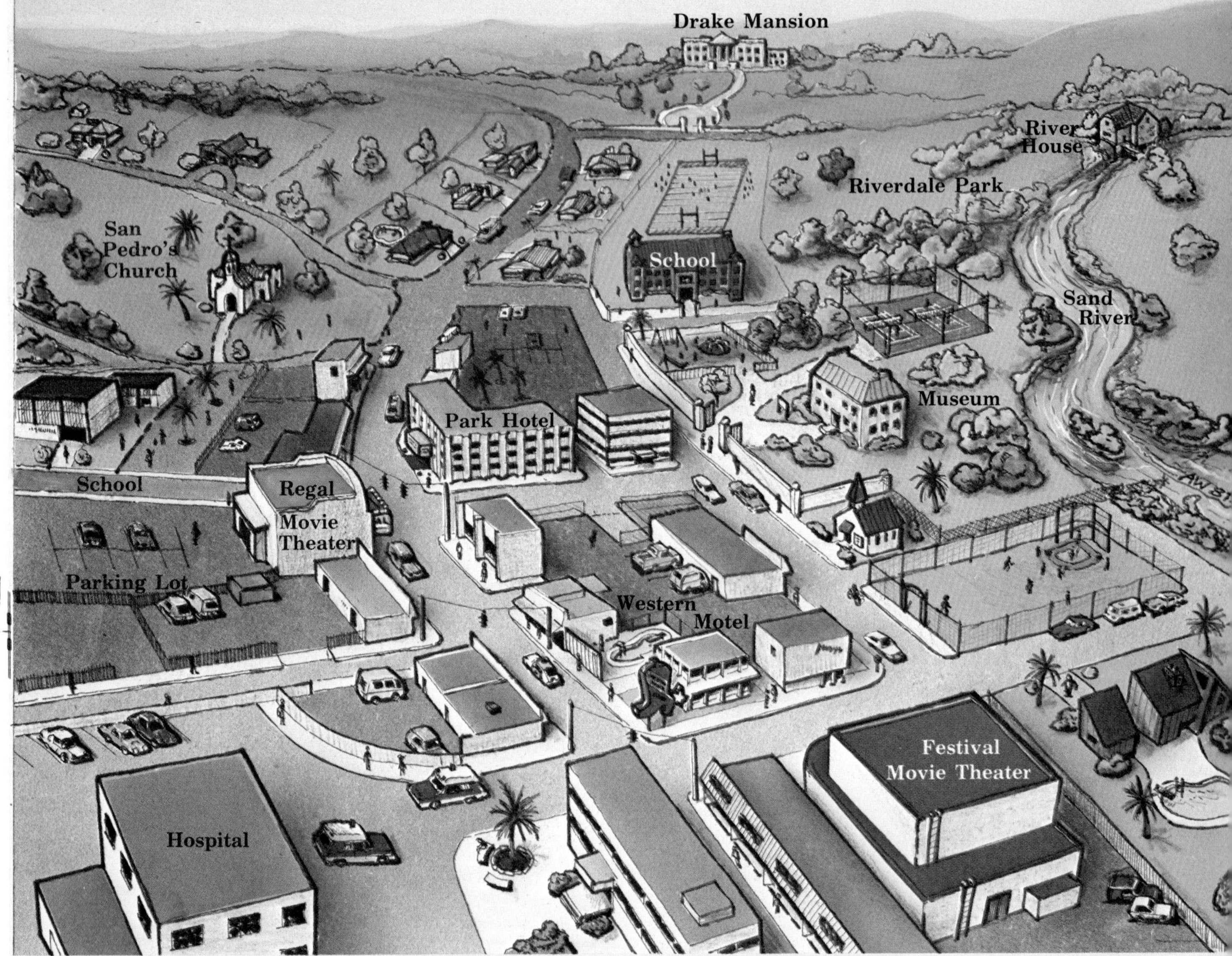

Riverdale, California is about fifty miles from Los Angeles, on the way to San Diego. It is also on the Sand River.

It is an old city. The big church on the hill, San Pedro, is two hundred years old. There are also some interesting old buildings in the center of the city.

Riverdale Park is near the river. There are trees and flowers in the park, and there is a small museum too. Children like the park a lot.

There are some interesting houses near Riverdale. Drake Mansion is three miles from the center of the city. It is a big, beautiful house on a hill. It is one hundred years old, and it is now the home of Buck Westwood, a famous movie star.

Penny Garland, a popular rock singer, is also from Riverdale. Her home, River House, is on the river, not far from the center of the city.

Penny and Buck are happy in Riverdale. Life is quiet, and people are friendly.

DO YOU UNDERSTAND?

1 Point to the map and say:

a. This is the Sand River.
b. This is San Pedro's Church.
c. This is Riverdale Park.
d. This is the museum.
e. This is Drake Mansion.
f. This is River House.

2 Say the names:

a. *It*'s two hundred years old.
b. *It*'s a building in the park.
c. *They* like the park.
d. *It*'s one hundred years old.
e. *He*'s a movie star.
f. *She*'s a rock singer.
g. *They*'re happy in Riverdale.

3 Answer the questions:

a. Where's Riverdale?
b. Where's San Pedro's Church?
c. How old is it?
d. Where's Riverdale Park?
e. Where's Drake Mansion?
f. Whose house is it?
g. Where's River House?
h. Whose house is it?
i. Who's Buck Westwood?
j. Who's Penny Garland?

Grammar

There is **There's**	a museum in Riverdale.
There are	**some** old houses in Riverdale.

Is there	a movie theater?	Yes, there is. No, there isn't.
Are there	**any** churches?	Yes, there are. No, there aren't.

1 Make true sentences:

a.

There's	a	museum school park	in the park. near the river. on a hill.
	an	old church old house	

b.

There are some	trees flowers cars children	in the park. in the parking lot.

2 Ask and answer the questions:

a.
S1: Is there a *hospital* near Riverdale Park?
S2: Yes, there is./No, there isn't.

b.

S1: Are there any	elephants horses lions trees flowers	in Riverdale Park?

S2: Yes, there are./No, there aren't.

7 Practice

How many lions are there?
There are two.

1 Find the animals. Tell a classmate:

S1: There's *a lion* in the picture.
S2: Where?
S1: Here.

2 Ask and answer the questions:

S1: How many *lions* are there?
S2: There are *two.*
S1: Where are they?
S2: Here and here.

3 Look at the map. Ask and answer the questions:

S1: Excuse me, please. Is there *a park* near here?
S2: Yes. There's one on *First* Street./No, there isn't.

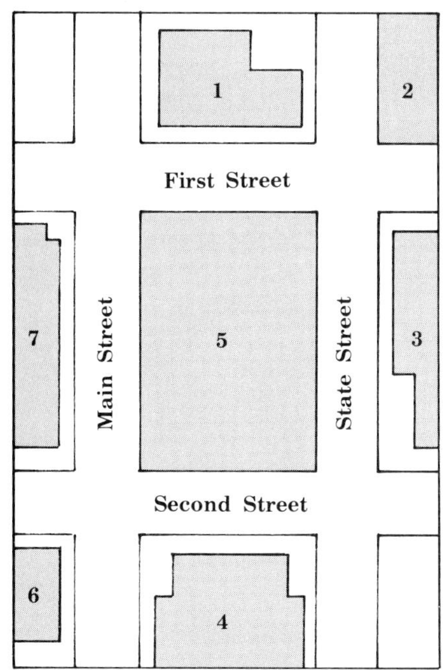

1 hotel
2 parking lot
3 hospital
4 church
5 park
6 bookstore
7 movie theater

4 Ask your classmates about places near your school:

S1: Is there *a movie theater* near here?
S2: Yes. There's one on *Main Street*./No, there isn't./ I don't know.

7

Review

Practice the conversations. Talk about different things on the map.

1
S1: Is there *a park* in Riverdale?
S2: Yes, there is.
S1: Where is it?
S2: It's *near the river.*

2
S1: Is there *a hospital* in Riverdale?
S2: Yes. It's here.
S1: Is there *a museum* too?
S2: Yes. The *museum* is here.

3
S1: How many *schools* are there in Riverdale?
S2: There are two.
S1: Where are they?
S2: There's one here, and there's one here.

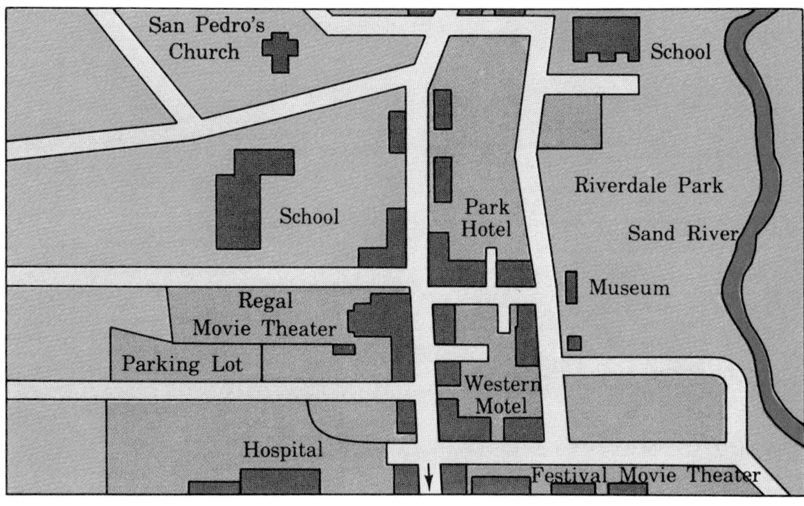

7
Reading

Happy families

What are their names?
How old are they?

This is a picture of the Kovic family. There are four children in this family—two boys and two girls. Their names are Jack, Mike, Linda and Mary. Their father's name is Frank, and their mother's name is Rose.

Mr. Kovic is forty-four years old, and Mrs. Kovic is forty. Mary is sixteen. Her sister is ten. Jack is fourteen, and his brother is twelve.

This is Jack on the bicycle. Linda is not very happy in this picture. There are some books in her hand. Are they her school books?

The Kovic family

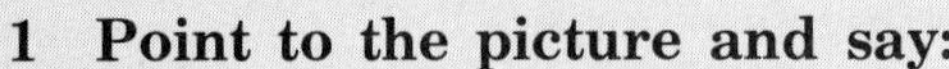

1 Point to the picture and say:

This is *Mr. Kovic. He*'s *forty-four* years old.

2 Ask and answer the questions:

a. How many boys are there in the Kovic family?
b. How many girls are there?
c. What's their father's name?
d. How old is their mother?
e. How old are Mike and Linda?

Listening

Look at the picture of the Cheng family.

1 Complete the table below:

Name:	Mr. Cheng	Mrs. Cheng	Sue	Tom	Lee
Age:					

2 Point to the picture and say:

This is *Mr. Cheng. He*'s .... years old.

The Cheng family

Small Talk

Talk about your brothers and sisters:

S1 (PETER): There are three children in my family—two girls and one boy.
S2: What are their names?
S1: Anne, Mary and Peter—that's me. How many children are there in your family?
S2: There's only one—that's me.

Writing

There are **some**	trees in the park.
There are**n't any**	

1 Look at Picture One and Picture Two. Complete the sentences:

a. How many women ..are.. there in Picture One? .... are three.
b. How .... women are .... in Picture Two? .... two.
c. .... buses are there in Picture One? There .... one.
d. .... buses .... in Picture Two? .... aren't any buses in Picture Two.

2 Write sentences about the pictures:

There are *ten cars* in Picture One, but there are *two cars* in Picture Two.

There is *one horse* in Picture Two, but there aren't any *horses* in Picture One.

Picture One Riverdale today

Picture Two Riverdale 70 years ago

Just for Fun

Ask questions like these:

How many thirteens are there in this box?
How many thirties are there?

13	17	50	80	50	80	14	90	70	13
30	90	17	16	90	17	90	17	30	50
14	14	90	70	13	80	50	19	50	40
40	17	50	17	15	70	13	17	16	13
15	50	16	60	17	70	18	80	19	90

8 A TALENT SHOW

1

JIM: Hey! Look at this. A talent show!
DEBBIE: Where?
JIM: Here. In the park. At the carnival.
TONY: The carnival? What carnival?
DEBBIE: Riverdale Carnival. It's on May first.
JIM: And there are prizes too. Look.
TONY: "First prize, $200." Not bad!

2

DEBBIE: What about your song, Tony? Sing it in the talent show.
TONY: OK. Good idea! Can you and Jim sing it with me?
JIM: Debbie can. She's a good singer.
TONY: What about you, Jim?
DEBBIE: He can't sing.

3

TONY: Oh. Can you play the guitar, Jim?
JIM: Yes, I can. Listen to this.

4

JIM: This little guitar is really good. Whose is it? Ringo's?
TONY: No. Ringo can't play the guitar.
DEBBIE: But he can play the drums. Listen!

DO YOU UNDERSTAND?

1 Right or wrong?

a. Riverdale Carnival is on May first.
b. There's a talent show at the carnival.
c. The first prize is $10.
d. Debbie can sing.
e. That's Ringo's guitar.
f. Ringo can't play the drums.

2 Say the names:

a. *His* song is great.
b. *He* can play the guitar.
c. *He* can sing.
d. *He* can't sing.
e. *She*'s a good singer.

3 Complete the sentences:

a. Debbie *can* sing.
b. She is a good ....
c. Tony can .... too.
d. Jim can play the ....
e. Ringo can play the ....

Grammar

<table>
<tr><td>Debbie</td><td>can</td><td colspan="2">sing.</td></tr>
<tr><td>Jim</td><td>cannot
can't</td><td colspan="2">sing.</td></tr>
<tr><td>Can</td><td>Jim
Debbie</td><td>play the guitar?</td><td>Yes, he can.
No, she can't.</td></tr>
</table>

1 Answer the questions:

a. Where's the carnival?
b. Is the carnival today?
c. Are there prizes for the talent show?
d. What's the first prize?
e. Who can't sing?
f. Who can sing?
g. Is that Ringo's guitar?
h. Whose guitar is it?

2 Ask and answer the questions:

<table>
<tr><td>S1: Can Tony</td><td>play the guitar
play the drums
sing</td><td>?</td></tr>
</table>

S2: Yes, *he* can./No, *he* can't./I don't know.

3 Make true sentences:

Tony Jim Debbie Ringo	can can't	play the guitar. play the drums. sing.

8 Practice

Sandy Larson is a wife and mother, and she is also a singer—a rock singer. All the young people really like her songs, and they think she is a great guitarist.

Richard Larson, her husband, is a swimming teacher at Madison High School. He is a good teacher and a good swimmer. But Richard is famous because he is a soccer player. He is the star of the New York Lions.

Their children, Jane, Daniel and Linda, cannot sing or play the guitar like their mother. But they are good at sports like their father. Jane and Daniel are very good baseball players. They are also good swimmers, and they can run fast. Linda is very good at tennis, and she is a good soccer player too.

1 Ask and answer the questions:

S1: Can *Daniel run fast?*
S2: Yes, *he* can.
S1: Can *Linda sing?*
S2: No, *she* can't.

2 Ask your classmates:

S1: Can you *play soccer?*
S2: Yes, I can.
S1: Are you a good *player?*
S2: Yes, I am./I'm OK./
No, I'm not.

or

S1: Can you *play soccer?*
S2: No, I can't.

NAME:	Kumi	Jill	Pedro
			✓
	✓		
		✓	
		✓	✓
	✓		
	✓		✓

3 Write about your classmates:

Pedro can play football.
Kumi can play soccer.
Jill cannot swim.

Review

8

Practice the conversations. Talk about Debbie, Jim, Anita and Tony.

1

S1: Who can *play the guitar?*
S2: *Tony* can.
S1: Can *he play the piano* too?
S2: No, *he* can't.

2

S1: Can *Debbie play the piano?*
S2: No, *she* can't, but *she* can *sing.*
S1: Can *she play the guitar* too?
S2: Yes, *she* can.

3

S1: *Anita* can *play the piano.*
And *she* can *sing* too!
S2: I know, but *she* can't *play the guitar.*

	Debbie	Jim	Anita	Tony
play the guitar	✓	✓		✓
play the piano		✓	✓	
sing	✓		✓	✓

8

Reading

Spacewoman and Zombo

Who are they?

Spacewoman is young, and she is very strong. She can fly like a bird. She can stop a car with one hand. She can stop that airplane. There are some dangerous men in it. The police cannot stop them, but Spacewoman can.

Spacewoman is smart, and she is friendly. She can help you with your problems.

Zombo is dangerous. Look at those hands! Look at that face!

Zombo is two hundred years old, but he is strong and smart. He can swim like a fish. He can kill a man with those hands. There are some policemen in that helicopter, but they cannot stop Zombo. Maybe Spacewoman can!

1 Answer the questions:

a. Who can stop a car with one hand?
b. Who can swim like a fish?
c. Who can fly like a bird?
d. Who can kill a man with his hands?
e. Who can help you with your problems?
f. How old is Zombo?

2 Ask and answer questions like this:

Is Spacewoman *friendly?*
Is Zombo *young?*

Use these words:

old, smart, strong, dangerous

Small Talk

Practice the conversations:

1

S1: Can you speak *Spanish?*
S2: Yes, I can./A little./No, I can't.

Note: See page 79 for other languages.

2

S1: Can you [ride a bicycle / swim / play *the guitar* / play *football*] ?

S2: Yes, I can./No, I can't.

Writing

Read about Jim:

This is Jim Marshall. He is fourteen years old, and he is a student at Riverdale High School. He is good at sports. He can play the guitar, and he is a good actor too.

1 Complete the letter:

April 15, 1984

Dear Mr. Westwood,

I really like your movies, and I want to be an actor like you. What can I do?

I am fourteen years ____, and I am a student at ______ ____ ______. I am good at ____. I can ____ ____ ______, and ___ ___ a good ______ too.

Can you help me? Thank you.

Sincerely,

Jim Marshall

2 Write a letter to a star about yourself.

Just for Fun

1 A riddle

What is the difference between a man and an elephant?

The answer is on page 86.

2 Choose a picture below. Ask and answer questions like this:

S1: This bird can't *fly*.
S2: Can it *swim?*
S1: Yes, it can.
S2: Is it the bird in Picture *Three?*
S1: Yes. That's right.

1		
2	✓	✓
3		✓
4	✓	✓
5	✓	
6	✓	

9 WHAT CAN YOU

1

1 *There are some letters in this square. Can you see them? What color are they?*

There are three letters in this square. They are the letters X, Y and Z. They are red. Some people cannot see these letters. They can see only one color in this square. They cannot see the difference between red and green.

2

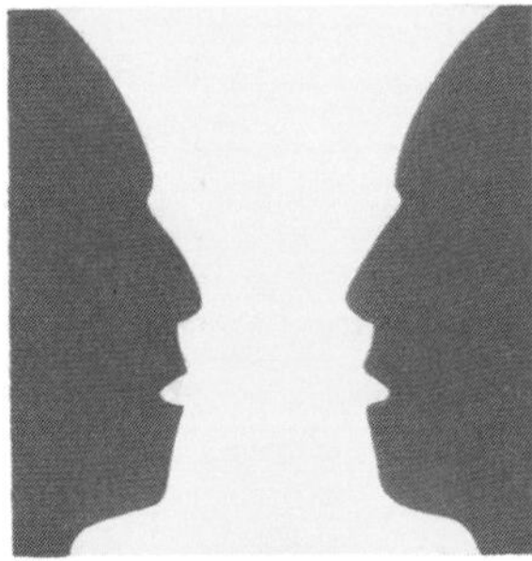

2 *What can you see in this square?*

This is a picture of a wine glass. Can you see it? It is yellow. There are two faces in this picture too. They are blue. Sometimes you can see the glass, and sometimes you can see the faces.

3

3 *How many boxes can you see here?*

Most people can see four boxes in this picture. Sometimes the boxes are yellow, blue and green. Sometimes the boxes are yellow, blue and red. They are not the same boxes.

4

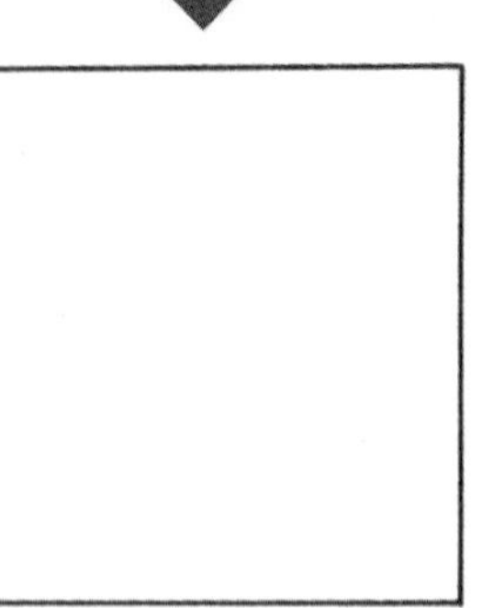

4 *Can you see a glass in this square?*

Look at Square Two again. Look at the glass, and count up to twenty. Then look at this white square and count up to five. Can you see a blue glass? Most people can.

SEE?

DO YOU UNDERSTAND?

1 Point to the pictures:

a. Some people can't see these letters.
b. This is a glass.
c. There are two faces in this picture.
d. Most people can see four boxes in this picture.
e. This square is white.

2 Answer the questions:

a. How many letters are there in Square One?
b. What color are the letters?
c. How many colors are there in Square Two?
d. How many boxes can you see in Square Three?
e. What colors are they?
f. Can you see a glass in Square Four?

3 Complete the sentences:

a. Some people cannot see the *letters* in Square One.
b. They cannot see the difference between .... and ....
c. Sometimes you can see a .... in Square Two.
d. Most people can see four .... in Square Three.
e. Most people can see a .... glass in Square Four.

Grammar

What can you see in this square?

There is a glass in this picture. Can you see **it?**
There are two faces in this picture. Can you see **them?**

Ask and answer the questions:

1
S1: Where's the *red Z?*
S2: It's in Square *One.*

2
S1: Where are the *blue faces?*
S2: They're in Square *Two.*

3
S1: What can you see in Square *One?*
S2: I can see *the letters X, Y and Z.*

4
S1: There's *a glass* in this picture. Can you see it?
S2: Yes. It's here.

5
S1: There are *three letters* in this picture. Can you see them?
S2: Yes. They're here, here and here./ No. I can't see them.

9
Practice

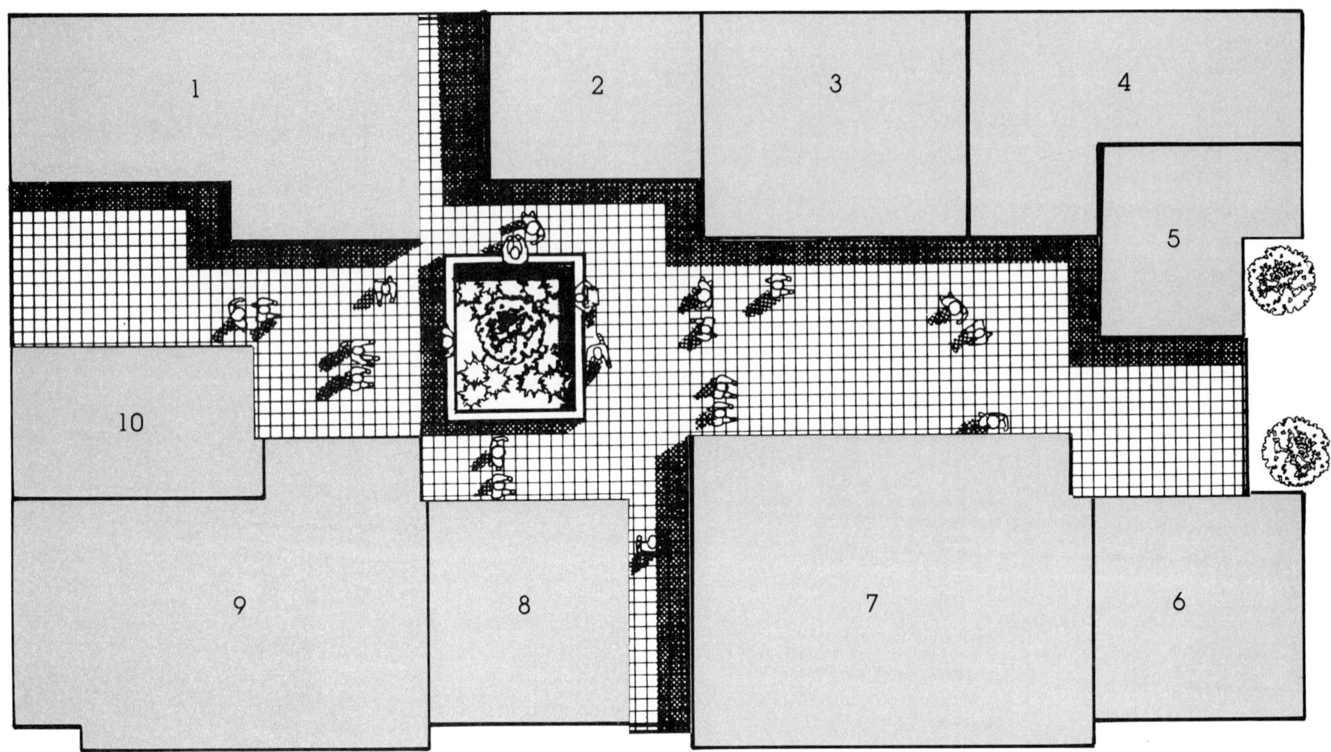

1 Ask and answer the questions:

a.
S1: There's *a movie theater* in the shopping center. Can you find it?
S2: Yes. Here it is.
or
No, I can't. Where is it?
S1: Here.

b.
S1: There are *two restaurants* in the shopping center. Can you find them?
S2: Yes. Here they are.
or
No, I can't. Where are they?
S1: Here and here.

c.
S1: What can you buy at *a record store?*
S2: You can buy *records*, of course!
S1: What else?
S2: You can buy *cassettes* too.

2 Ask your classmates:

a.
S1: Where's my *pen?* I can't find it.
S2: I think it's *in your book.*
S1: Oh, thanks.

b.
S1: Where are my *books?* I can't find them.
S2: I think they're *on your desk.*
S1: Oh, thanks.

1 Blue Cross Shoe Store
men's shoes
women's shoes

2 The Ice Cream Place
ice cream
cookies

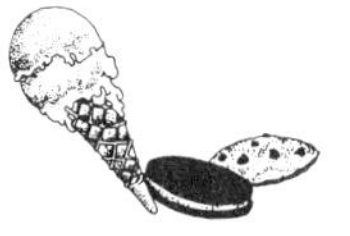

3 Disco Record Store
records
cassettes

4 Corner Bookstore
books
newspapers
magazines

5 The Mayfair Restaurant
Open 7 A.M. — 3 P.M.

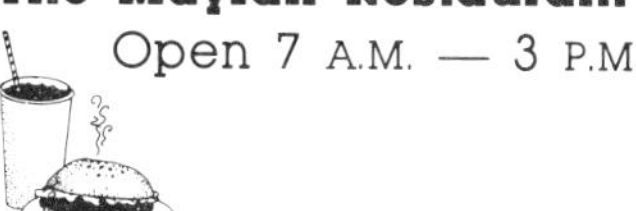

6 Penny's Shoes
women's shoes
purses

7 Parkway Movie Theater

8 Brooks Clothing Store
women's clothes

9 Portney's Restaurant
Open 12 P.M. — 11 P.M.

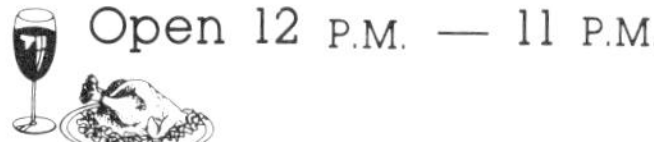

10 Ralph's Clothing Store
men's clothing

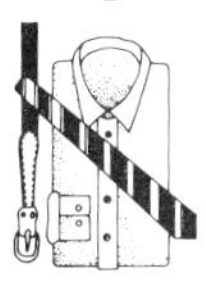

Review

9

Practice the conversations. Talk about different things in the picture.

Picasso: *Three Musicians*

1

S1: There's *a guitar* in this picture. Can you see it?
S2: Yes, I can. It's here.
S1: That's right.

2

S1: There are *two hats* in this picture.
S2: I can't see them. Where are they?
S1: Look. They're here and here.
S2: Oh. I can see them now.

3

S1: There are *seven eyes* in this picture.
S2: *Seven?* I can only see *six.*
S1: Count them.
S2: *One, two, three, four, five, six, seven.* Yes, you're right.

9 Reading

Can animals see colors?

Colors are not important for some animals. They cannot see the difference between red, green, yellow and blue. Horses and elephants, for example, cannot see colors.

Most people, however, can see colors. Chimpanzees and monkeys are like people. They can see the difference between red, green, yellow and blue. The octopus can see these colors too. Its eyes are very good. Colors are also important for birds and most fish. They can see a lot of different colors.

1 Right or wrong?

a. Horses can see colors.
b. Monkeys can see the difference between red and green.
c. The octopus can see colors.
d. Fish can't see colors.

2 Make true sentences:

Chimpanzees Most fish Birds Some animals The octopus	can can't	see colors.

Listening

Answer the question:

Bees are insects. There is a bee on this flower. Can it see the color of the flower?

Small Talk

Practice the conversation:

S1: How many *hats* can you see in this picture?
S2: I can see *four*. How many can you see?
S1: I can see *four* too.
or
I can see *five*.

Writing

Read Jack's note:

4/30
Paul,
I can't play football with you at 4:00.
Can we play at 6:00?
Call me at home.
Jack

Write a note to a friend.
You can use these words:

play *tennis*
go to the movies
go to the park

Just for Fun

Complete the words.
Say the numbers and spell them:

1st	2nd	3rd	4th	5th
f i r st	s __ c __ nd	__ hi __ d	fo __ r __ __	__ i __ th

6th	7th	8th	9th	10th
si __ __ h	se __ __ nt __	ei __ __ th	n __ n __ __	te __ __ __

10 WHAT ARE YOU

1

Today is Saturday, May first. It is the day of the Riverdale Carnival. It is two o'clock. Tony is at home. Jim and Debbie are with him. They are singing Tony's song. Tony's sister, Anita, is listening to them. Ringo is sitting next to her.

ANITA: That's a good song, Tony. I like it.
TONY: It's not bad.
DEBBIE: We like it too.
JIM: I think it's great.

2

ANITA: Look at Ringo. What's he doing?
TONY: He's dancing.
JIM: And he's playing the drums too. He's really good.

3

DEBBIE: It's four o'clock, Tony. Let's sing the song again.
TONY: Be quiet, Ringo. You can't play with us now.

4

TONY: What time is it?
DEBBIE: Oh! It's five o'clock.
JIM: Come on. Let's go to the carnival.
DEBBIE: Can Ringo come with us?
TONY: OK. Take the little guitar to the car, Ringo.
ANITA: Goodbye! Good luck!

DOING?

DO YOU UNDERSTAND?

1 Right or wrong?

a. The carnival is on Monday.
b. Anita is singing Tony's song.
c. Ringo is sitting next to Anita.
d. Ringo can sing.
e. He can dance.
f. Debbie and Jim like Tony's song.

2 Say the names:

a. *She*'s listening to Tony's song.
b. *He*'s at home.
c. *He*'s playing the drums.
d. *She*'s Tony's sister.
e. *They*'re going to the carnival.

3 Point to the pictures:

a. It's two o'clock.
b. It's three o'clock.
c. It's four o'clock.
d. It's five o'clock.

Grammar

What time is it?	It is It's	two o'clock.

What is What's	he doing?	He is He's	playing the guitar.
What are	they doing?	They are They're	singing.

I	am	at home.	Anita is with	**me.**
He	is			**him.**
She				**her.**
We	are			**us.**
You				**you.**
They				**them.**

1 What time is it?

a. Tony is singing with Debbie and Jim.
b. Ringo is playing the drums.
c. They're going to the carnival.

2 Ask and answer the questions:

a. What are Debbie and Tony doing in Picture One?
b. What are Jim and Tony doing?
c. What's Anita doing?
d. What's Ringo doing in Picture Two?
e. Where are the people going in Picture Four?

3 Complete the sentences with pronouns:

a. Debbie and Jim are with him . (Tony)
b. Anita is listening to .... (Jim, Debbie and Tony)
c. Ringo is sitting next to .... (Anita)
d. Debbie is singing with .... (Tony)

10 Practice

1 These people are talking on the telephone. What else are they doing?

S1: What's *he* doing?
S2: *He*'s *writing a letter.*

What are you doing?
I'm making dinner.

2 Practice the telephone conversation:

S1: Hello.
S2: Hi, *Maria.* This is *Mike.*
S1: Oh, hi, *Mike.* How are you?
S2: Fine. And you?
S1: I'm fine.
S2: What are you doing?
S1: I'm *making dinner.* What about you?
S2: I'm *writing a letter.*
S1: Can I come over?
S2: Sure.
S1: OK. Bye.
S2: Bye.

Note: "Can I come over?" means "Can I go to your house?"

3 Now talk to a friend on the telephone. Follow the conversation above.

1

Kim/watching TV

2

Mike/writing a letter

Maria/making dinner

3

Ellen/reading the newspaper

José/playing the piano

Review

10

Practice the conversations. Use different pictures.

1

S1: What time is it?
S2: It's *eight* o'clock.
S1: Where's *Jim?*
S2: *He's in Riverdale.*
S1: Is *Debbie* with *him?*
S2: Yes, *she* is.

2

S1: What's *Debbie* doing?
S2: *She's studying English.*
S1: Is *Tony* with *her?*
S2: No, *he* isn't.

3

S1: What time is it?
S2: It's *five* o'clock.
S1: Where are *Jim and Debbie?*
S2: They're *at home.*
S1: What are they doing?
S2: They're *doing their homework.*

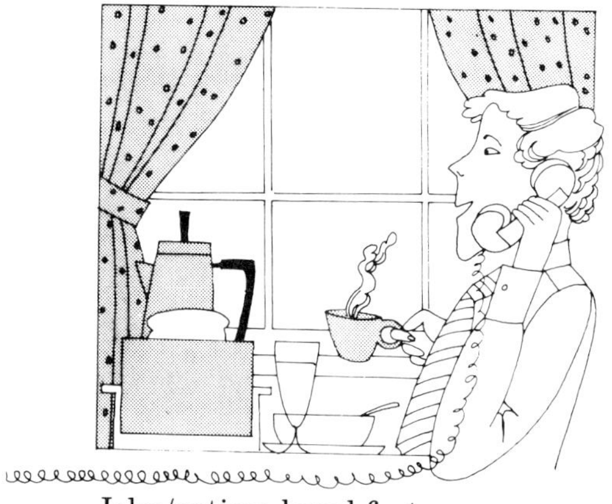

John/eating breakfast

4

Joe/reading a book

Paul/playing the guitar

10

Reading

Ringo's dreams

Ringo is very smart. Sometimes he is just like a little boy. Look at him now. He is asleep. Maybe he is dreaming. Maybe he is doing a lot of great things in his dream. Sweet dreams, Ringo!

I'm smart. I'm strong and handsome. I'm Superchimp. I'm flying to Hollywood. I want to be a movie star. I'm flying up and up. It's easy. It's great!

Oh! What's that? It's Zombo's airplane. He's dangerous. He can kill me. Help! Police! I'm going down and down . . . and down!

Where am I? I'm sitting on the ground. What am I doing here? I'm not flying now. I can't really fly. I can fly in my dreams, but I can't fly in real life.

Point to the pictures. Make true sentences:

In real life In his dream	Ringo	is asleep. is sitting on a chair. is flying. is strong. is handsome.

Small Talk

Tim is sitting	in front of behind next to	Mary. Jim. Isabel. John.

Practice the conversation:

S1: Where's Tim sitting?
S2: He's sitting *in front of Mary.*
S1: What about Anne? Where's she sitting?
S2: She's . . .

Writing

Who is this? What is he doing?

1 Write about Ringo and his dream:

In real life he is Ringo. He *is* .... young chimpanzee. He is .... home. He .... on a chair, and he .... looking at a newspaper.

But in his dream he is Swinging Sam. He is .... rock star, and .... in Hollywood.

2 Talk and write about yourself and your dreams:

In real life I am . . .
But in my dreams I am . . .

Just for Fun

Guess what your classmate is doing:

S1: What's *he* doing?
S2: Is *he riding a horse?*
S1: No, *he* isn't.
S2: Is *he playing the guitar?*
S1: Yes, *he* is.

11 THE OK CORRAL

1 *What are these men doing?*

It is October 26, 1881. These men are in Tombstone, Arizona. They are standing near the OK Corral and talking. They are talking about Wyatt Earp, the sheriff of Tombstone. They want to kill him.

2 *Who are these men?*

This is Wyatt Earp and his two brothers. They are looking for the outlaws—the Clanton brothers and the McLaury brothers.

3 *There are the outlaws! Are they leaving?*

No! They are waiting for Wyatt Earp. Their hands are on their guns. The Earp brothers are walking toward them. Wyatt is shouting, "Drop your guns, and put up your hands!"

4 *What is happening?*

Suddenly, the men are fighting. The Earp brothers are killing the outlaws. Some of the men are on the ground. One of them is running away. Are the Earp brothers dead or alive?

DO YOU UNDERSTAND?

1 Right or wrong?

a. The Clanton brothers and the McLaury brothers are outlaws.
b. The Earp brothers are outlaws.
c. The Earp brothers are running away.

2 Which picture?

a. The Earp brothers are looking for the outlaws.
b. Wyatt Earp is talking to the outlaws.
c. The outlaws are on the ground.
d. One of the outlaws is running away.

3 Complete the sentences:

a. The outlaws are standing near the OK Corral.
b. They're .... about Wyatt Earp.
c. The Earp brothers are .... for the outlaws.
d. The outlaws are .... for Wyatt Earp.

Grammar

These men are	talking.	
They are not They aren't	leaving.	
Are they	fighting?	Yes, they are. No, they aren't.

What is What's	happening?

1 Make true sentences:

The outlaws The Earp brothers	are	standing near the OK Corral. talking. looking for the outlaws. waiting for the Earps. killing the outlaws.

2 Ask about the Earp brothers and the outlaws:

S1: What are the *outlaws* doing in Picture *One?*
S2: They're *standing near the OK Corral and talking.*

11 Practice

Sally Davis

7:00
Study with Joe for math test

9:00
Talk to Mr. Brager

5:00? 6:00?
make dinner for Dad's birthday

8:00
Dad's dinner

Write to Josie!

Alice Davis

9:00 – 4:00
Work

5:00
Tennis

8:00
Dan - birthday dinner

10:00
Studio 50 – dancing

Dan Davis

9:00 – 3:00
Work

5:00
Tennis

8:00
Dinner

10:00
Dancing at Studio 50

1 Ask and answer the questions:

a.

S1: What's *Sally* doing?
S2: I don't know. What time is it?
S1: It's *seven* o'clock.
S2: Oh, *she*'s *studying with Joe.*

b.

S1: What are *Dan and Alice* doing?
S2: I don't know. What time is it?
S1: It's *ten* o'clock.
S2: Oh, they're *dancing at Studio 50.*

2 Now ask about your classmate's family:

S1: What's your *mother* doing?
S2: I don't know. What time is it?
S1: It's *six* o'clock.
S2: Well, *she*'s probably *making dinner.*

Fred Davis

9:00 – 4:00
School

5:00
Practice my guitar

6:00
Watch "Postman"
Channel 8

Study!

3 **Complete the note. Use contractions when you can.**

Marty– 5/22

I'm studying at John's house. We ___ working on the history project. ___ you working on that project too? Ann ___ coming over at 5:00. She ___ making ice cream. Please come.

Sara

11

Review

Practice the conversations. Use different pictures.

1

S1: Which picture are you looking at?
S2: Number *one.*
S1: Oh, yes. It's a picture of some *children.* What are they doing?
S2: *They're playing games.*

2

S1: What's happening in this picture?
S2: Which picture?
S1: Number *two.*
S2: Some *women* are *dancing.*

3

S1: Are these *men playing soccer?*
S2: Yes.
S1: And what about these *soldiers?*
S2: They're *fighting.*

11 Reading

Gunfight at the OK Corral

Which picture is the reading about?

This is a picture of the famous gunfight at the OK Corral in Tombstone, Arizona. Wyatt Earp and his brothers are on the left, and the four outlaws are on the right. They are fighting. Two outlaws are dead, and one is falling to the ground. One outlaw is running away. There are also two Earp brothers on the ground, but they are alive.

Wyatt Earp is standing in the middle of the street. He is looking at the men on the ground. You can see his empty gun in his hand.

1 Answer the questions about the reading:

a. How many men are on the ground?
b. How many men are dead? Who are they?
c. How many men are alive? Who are they?

2 Point to:

a. Wyatt Earp's brothers
b. the outlaws
c. the dead men
d. Wyatt Earp

Listening

Answer the question:

What is Old Joe looking at—Picture One, Picture Two or Picture Three?

Small Talk

Practice the conversation:

S1: When's your birthday?
S2: It's in *March*.
S1: Which day?
S2: The *second*. When's your birthday?
S1: It's on *November fifth*.

Writing

**Are these people spies?
What are they doing?**

1 Is the woman listening to the radio, or is she taking a picture?
2 Is the girl writing a letter, or is she drawing a map?
3 Is the man reading a newspaper, or is he talking to the old woman?
4 Is the boy reading a book, or is he looking at the boats?
5 Is the dog playing a game, or is it taking a letter to those men?

Make sentences like this:

The woman is not really listening to the radio. She is taking a picture.

Just for Fun

1 A riddle

What is this?

It has four legs, but it cannot run.
The answer is on page 86.

2 How many words can you make with the letters in these words?

IMPORTANT	ELEPHANT
1 man	1 hat
2 it	2 ....
3	3 ....

12 CARNIVAL DAY

1

It is Carnival Day in Riverdale. There are a lot of people in the park. They are listening to a woman with a microphone. Her name is Penny Garland. She is a rock singer. Tony, Debbie and Jim are standing behind her.

PENNY: And now here's a new group with a new song. They're Tony, Jim and Debbie—the Riverdale Rockers. The song is "That's Life." OK, Tony? Let's go.

2

PENNY: Hey! What's going on here? Whose chimpanzee is that?

3

TONY: Go away, Ringo! You can't play with us.

4

PENNY: I see. It's Tony's chimp. His name is Ringo. Can you play the drums, Ringo?

JIM: Yes, he can.

PENNY: OK. Let's listen to Tony's song again—with Ringo on the drums!

5

PENNY: Here's Buck Westwood, your favorite movie star. And he's giving first prize to the Riverdale Rockers—and Ringo.

BUCK: Fantastic! That's a great song. And I like your drummer. He's a real star!

DO YOU UNDERSTAND?

1 Right or wrong?

a. The carnival is in Riverdale Park.
b. Penny Garland is a movie star.
c. Tony's song is "I Like It."
d. Ringo is a good drummer.
e. Buck Westwood is a movie star.

2 Say the names:

a. The people in the park are listening to *her.*
b. Penny is standing in front of *them.*
c. Jim and Debbie are singing with *him.*
d. Buck is giving *them* first prize.

3 Answer the questions:

a. Where are the people?
b. What's the name of the group?
c. What's the name of their song?
d. What's Ringo playing?
e. What's Buck giving to the Riverdale Rockers?

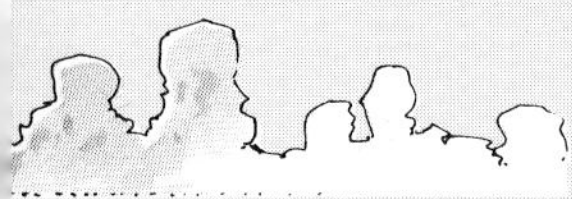

Grammar

1 Point to the pictures. Make true sentences:

Ringo Penny Debbie Jim Tony Buck	is standing	next to near in front of behind	Ringo. Penny. Debbie. Jim. Tony. Buck.

2 Ask and answer the questions:

a.

S1: How many *people* are there in Picture *Three?*
S2: There *are two.*

b.

S1: Can *Penny*	sing play the guitar play the drums	?

S2: Yes, *she* can./No, *she* can't./I don't know.

3 Complete the sentences:

a. There are a lot of people in the park.
b. The people .... listening to Penny.
c. Penny is a rock ....
d. Jim is .... behind Penny.
e. Ringo can .... the drums.
f. Buck Westwood is .... movie star.

12 Practice

1 Who is it?

S1: *She*'s wearing *a red dress and a green belt.*
S2: *Grace.*
S1: Right.

2 You are the people in the picture. Ask and answer the questions:

a.

PEGGY: Grace, where's my *red purse?*
GRACE: It's *in* your *closet.*

b.

PHIL: Fred, where are my *brown pants?*
FRED: Are they *in* your *closet?*
PHIL: No.
FRED: Are they *on* your *bed?*
PHIL: Oh, yes. Here they are. Thanks.

Review

Practice the conversations. Use different pictures.

1

S1: What's *Debbie* doing?
S2: *She's playing soccer.*
S1: Is *Jim* with *her?*
S2: No, *he* isn't. *He's riding a horse.*

2

S1: Can you see *Ringo?*
S2: Yes. *He's* over there.
S1: I can't see *him.*
S2: *He's* with those *boys and girls.* They're *singing and playing the guitar.*

3

S1: Where's *Tony?*
S2: *He's dancing.*
S1: I can't see *him.*
S2: Look! *He's* over there in the *green* hat.

4

S1: What are those *boys and girls* doing?
S2: They're *riding horses.*
S1: Is *Tony* with them?
S2: No, *he* isn't. *He's dancing.*

3 Talk on the telephone to a classmate. You are spies.

X-10: Hello, *Zero-4?*
ZERO-4: Yes?
X-10: This is *X-10.* Can you meet me *at the Plaza* at *4:00?*
ZERO-4: Yes. What are you wearing?
X-10: I'm wearing *jeans and a black shirt.*
ZERO-4: OK. Bye.

12

Reading

Two stars from Riverdale

What are their names?
What are they interested in?

Buck Westwood is a tall, handsome movie star. He is forty years old, and he is a good actor. His movies are very popular in the United States.

Buck is interested in a lot of things—animals, art and music, for example. His house, Drake Mansion, is on a hill near the Sand River, three miles from Riverdale. It is one hundred years old, and there is a lot of land behind it. There are a lot of interesting things in the house and on the land.

Penny Garland, the rock star, is from Riverdale too. Her home, River House, is on the river, not far from the center of the city.

Penny is twenty-five years old. She is a famous singer and song writer. She is very intelligent too. She can speak French, Spanish and Chinese. She is also interested in cars and airplanes. She is a very good driver, and she can fly an airplane. There are some interesting airplanes at her house.

1 Ask and answer the questions:

a. Who's Buck Westwood?
b. Where's his house?
c. Who's Penny Garland?
d. What can she do?

2 Make true sentences:

a.

Buck Penny	is	forty. handsome. tall. twenty-five. a singer. a song writer. an actor.

b.

Buck Penny	is interested in	music. art. cars. airplanes.

Small Talk

Practice the conversation:

S1: Hi! Where are you going?
S2: To *the movies.* Can you come with me?
S1: Sorry. Not now.
S2: Why not?
S1: I'm going to *the carnival.*

the store	the circus
the park	the football game
the museum	church
the library	school

Writing

1 Ask a friend:

How old are you?
What are you interested in?
What are you good at?
What languages can you speak?
Can you *swim?*

2 Write about your friend like this:

Joan is .... old. She .... interested in .... She .... good at .... can ....

3 Now write about yourself.

Just for Fun

1 Guess the word:

C _ _ _ _ _ _ _ _ _

S1: There are *ten* letters in this word.
S2: What's the first letter?
S1: It's "*C.*"
S2: What's the *second* letter?
S1: It's "*H.*"
S2: What's the *tenth* letter?
S1: "*E.*"
S2: Is the word *"chimpanzee"?*
S1: Yes. That's right!

2 Can you remember? (A quiz)

a. Is a dolphin a fish? (Unit 1)
b. What is the name of Jim's English teacher? (Unit 2)
c. Whose sister is an English teacher? (Unit 2)
d. How old is Jim? (Unit 5)
e. Where is Carlos da Costa from? (Unit 6)
f. Where is Penny Garland's house? (Unit 7)
g. Who can play the piano? (Unit 8)
h. What is the name of Tony's song? (Unit 12)

ADDITIONAL DIALOGS FOR THE REVIEW SECTION

Unit 1, page 5

1
S1: What's this?
S2: It's a fish.

2
S1: Is this a dolphin?
S2: Yes, it is.
S1: And what's this?
S2: It's a snake.

3
S1: Is this a man?
S2: No, it isn't.
S1: What is it?
S2: It's a woman.

Unit 2, page 11

1
S1: Who's that?
S2: That's Debbie.
She's a student.
S1: Thanks.

2
S1: This is Anita's brother.
S2: What's his name?
S1: Tony.

3
S1: Is Anita a teacher?
S2: Yes, she is.
S1: Is her brother a teacher too?
S2: No, he isn't.

Unit 3, page 17

1
S1: Look! A snake!
S2: A snake? Where?
S1: Under that bag.
S2: Which bag?
S1: The white bag.

2
S1: Is that a snake?
S2: Where?
S1: In the black bag.
S2: Yes! Run!

3
S1: Hey! What's that?
S2: It's a snake.
S1: Really?
S2: Yes. It's a green snake.

Unit 4, page 23

1
S1: Who are those boys?
S2: They're singers.
They're from Greece.

2
S1: Where are those girls from?
S2: Brazil.
S1: They're good guitarists!

3
S1: Are those boys from Spain?
S2: Yes, they are.
S1: Are they singers?
S2: No, they aren't. They're guitarists.

Unit 5, page 29

1
S1: Hey! Look at the swimmers. What are their names?
S2: Pat and Mandy.
S1: Are they English or American?
S2: American.

2
S1: Look! Kay and June!
S2: Who are they?
S1: They're English tennis players.
S2: They're great!

3
S1: Bill and Andy are great gymnasts!
S2: Where are they from?
S1: They're from England.

Unit 6, page 35

1
S1: Whose car is that?
S2: Which car?
S1: The red car.
S2: It's Linda's.

2
S1: Is that your car?
S2: Which car?
S1: The white car.
S2: No, my car is blue.
That's Kathy's car.

3
S1: Is that Kathy's car?
S2: Which car?
S1: The black car.
S2: No, that's Tom's.

4
S1: Who's that man in the green car?
S2: That's Tony.
S1: Is he English?
S2: No. He's American.
S1: What city is he from?
S2: I don't know.

Unit 7, page 41

1
S1: Is there a museum in Riverdale?
S2: Yes, there is.
S1: Where is it?
S2: It's near the river.

2
S1: Is there a hotel in Riverdale?
S2: Yes. It's here.
S1: Is there a church too?
S2: Yes. The church is here.

3
S1: How many movie theaters are there in Riverdale?
S2: There are two.
S1: Where are they?
S2: There's one here, and there's one here.

Unit 8, page 47

1
S1: Who can play the piano?
S2: Anita can.
S1: Can she play the guitar too?
S2: No, she can't.

2
S1: Can Tony play the piano?
S2: No, he can't, but he can play the guitar.
S1: Can he sing too?
S2: Yes, he can.

3
S1: Jim can play the guitar. And he can play the piano too!
S2: I know, but he can't sing.

Unit 9, page 53

1
S1: There's a book in this picture. Can you see it?
S2: Yes, I can. It's here.
S1: That's right.

2
S1: There are five faces in this picture.
S2: I can't see them. Where are they?
S1: Look. They're here, here, . . . and here.
S2: Oh. I can see them now.

3
S1: There are six hands in this picture.
S2: Six? I can only see four.
S1: Count them.
S2: One, two, three, four, five, six. Yes, you're right.

Unit 10, page 59

1
S1: What time is it?
S2: It's ten o'clock.
S1: Where's Debbie?
S2: She's at school.
S1: Is Jim with her?
S2: Yes, he is.

2
S1: What's Jim doing?
S2: He's doing his homework.
S1: Is Tony with him?
S2: No, he isn't.

3
S1: What time is it?
S2: It's seven o'clock.
S1: Where are Debbie and Jim?
S2: They're at Tony's house.
S1: What are they doing?
S2: They're singing.

Unit 11, page 65

1
S1: Which picture are you looking at?
S2: Number two.
S1: Oh, yes. It's a picture of some women. What are they doing?
S2: They're dancing.

2
S1: What's happening in this picture?
S2: Which picture?
S1: Number three.
S2: Some men are playing soccer.

3
S1: Are these soldiers fighting?
S2: Yes.
S1: And what about these children?
S2: They're playing games.

Unit 12, page 71

1
S1: What's Ringo doing?
S2: He's singing.
S1: Is Tony with him?
S2: No, he isn't.
He's dancing.

2
S1: Can you see Tony?
S2: Yes. He's over there.
S1: I can't see him.
S2: He's with those boys and girls. They're dancing.

3
S1: Where's Jim?
S2: He's riding a horse.
S1: I can't see him.
S2: Look! He's over there in the yellow hat.

4
S1: What are those boys and girls doing?
S2: They're singing and playing the guitar.
S1: Is Debbie with them?
S2: No, she isn't. She's playing soccer.

LISTENING TEXTS

Unit 1, page 6

A
It isn't an octopus.
It isn't a shark.
What is it?
B
Is it a dolphin?
No, it isn't.
Is it a snake?
No!
What is it?
C
It isn't an octopus.
It isn't a snake.
What is it?
D
Is it an elephant?
No!
Is it an animal?
No!
What is it?

Unit 3, page 18

JIM: Where is the key?
FRIEND: It's in the bag.
JIM: No, it isn't.
FRIEND: No?
JIM: No.
FRIEND: Where is it? Is it under the table?
JIM: No, it isn't.
FRIEND: Well, where *is* it? . . . Oh, I know. It's in your pocket.
JIM: Right!

Unit 5, page 30

MIKE: How old are you, John?
JOHN: I'm nineteen.
MIKE: Look at these squares. Where's the number nineteen?
JOHN: It's in Squares Two, Three and Five.
MIKE: Add up the first numbers in those squares.
JOHN: Two and one are three. Three and sixteen are nineteen.
MIKE: That's right. The answer is nineteen. That's your age. Right?
JOHN: Right. What about you, Mike? How old are you?
MIKE: My age is in Squares Three and Five.

Unit 7, page 42

Hello. My name is Sue—Sue Cheng. This is a picture of me and my family. That's me with my bicycle.

There are three children in my family—two boys and a girl. My brothers' names are Tom and Lee. Tom is thirteen years old, and Lee is eleven. My father is forty-two, and my mother is thirty-nine. I'm fifteen.

Unit 9, page 54

Most animals can't see colors. What about insects? Their eyes aren't like the eyes of people, but most insects can see colors. The color of flowers is very important for some insects. Bees, for example, can see a lot of different colors.

Unit 11, page 66

WILL: What's happening now, Old Joe?
OLD JOE: There are five men on the ground, and there are three more men out there.
WILL: What are they doing?
OLD JOE: I think they're helping the Earp brothers.
WILL: The Earp brothers aren't dead?
OLD JOE: Nope. Three of the Clantons are dead, but the Earps are alive.
WILL: Where's Wyatt?
OLD JOE: I don't know. Oh, yeah. There he is. He's walking away!

USEFUL VOCABULARY

Days of the Week

Sunday	Wednesday	Friday
Monday	Thursday	Saturday
Tuesday		

Months of the Year

January	May	September
February	June	October
March	July	November
April	August	December

Cardinal Numbers

1 one	11 eleven	21 twenty-one
2 two	12 twelve	22 twenty-two
3 three	13 thirteen	30 thirty
4 four	14 fourteen	40 forty
5 five	15 fifteen	50 fifty
6 six	16 sixteen	60 sixty
7 seven	17 seventeen	70 seventy
8 eight	18 eighteen	80 eighty
9 nine	19 nineteen	90 ninety
10 ten	20 twenty	100 a/one hundred

Ordinal Numbers

1st first	11th eleventh	21st twenty-first
2nd second	12th twelfth	22nd twenty-second
3rd third	13th thirteenth	30th thirtieth
4th fourth	14th fourteenth	40th fortieth
5th fifth	15th fifteenth	50th fiftieth
6th sixth	16th sixteenth	60th sixtieth
7th seventh	17th seventeenth	70th seventieth
8th eighth	18th eighteenth	80th eightieth
9th ninth	19th nineteenth	90th ninetieth
10th tenth	20th twentieth	100th hundredth

The Family

Male	Female	Plural
grandfather	grandmother	grandparents
father	mother	parents
son	daughter	children
grandson	granddaughter	grandchildren
brother	sister	brothers and sisters
uncle	aunt	uncles and aunts
nephew	niece	nieces and nephews
cousin	cousin	cousins
husband	wife	

Colors

black	brown
white	orange
red	purple
green	pink
blue	gray
yellow	beige

Clothes

Men's and Women's

belt
coat
gloves
hat
jacket
jeans
pants
shoes
shorts
sneakers
socks
suit
sweater
T-shirt

Men's

shirt
sports coat
tie

Underclothes
underwear (briefs, shorts)
undershirt

Women's

blouse
dress
purse
skirt

Underclothes
bra
pantyhose
slip
stockings
underwear (underpants)

Countries	Nationalities	Languages
Argentina	Argentinian	Spanish
Australia	Australian	English
Austria	Austrian	German
Belgium	Belgian	Flemish, Dutch, French
Bolivia	Bolivian	Spanish
Brazil	Brazilian	Portuguese
Canada	Canadian	English, French
Chile	Chilean	Spanish
China	Chinese	Chinese
Colombia	Colombian	Spanish
Costa Rica	Costa Rican	Spanish
Cuba	Cuban	Spanish
Czechoslovakia	Czech	Czech, Slovak
Denmark	Danish	Danish
The Dominican Republic	Dominican	Spanish
Ecuador	Ecuadorean	Spanish
Egypt	Egyptian	Arabic
El Salvador	Salvadorean	Spanish
Finland	Finnish	Finnish, Swedish
France	French	French
Germany	German	German
Great Britain	British	English
Greece	Greek	Greek
Guatemala	Guatemalan	Spanish
Haiti	Haitian	French
Honduras	Honduran	Spanish
India	Indian	Hindi, English
Indonesia	Indonesian	Bahasa Indonesian
Iran	Iranian	Persian
Iraq	Iraqi	Arabic
Israel	Israeli	Hebrew, Arabic
Italy	Italian	Italian
Japan	Japanese	Japanese
Jordan	Jordanian	Arabic
Korea	Korean	Korean
Laos	Laotian	Lao
Lebanon	Lebanese	Arabic
Mexico	Mexican	Spanish
The Netherlands	Dutch	Dutch
Nicaragua	Nicaraguan	Spanish
Nigeria	Nigerian	English
Norway	Norwegian	Norwegian
Pakistan	Pakistani	Urdu, Punjabi, English
Panama	Panamanian	Spanish
Peru	Peruvian	Spanish
The Philippines	Filipino	Pilipino, English, Spanish
Poland	Polish	Polish
Portugal	Portuguese	Portuguese
Saudi Arabia	Saudi Arabian	Arabic
The Soviet Union	Soviet or Russian	Russian
Spain	Spanish	Spanish
Sweden	Swedish	Swedish
Switzerland	Swiss	French, German, Italian
Syria	Syrian	Arabic
Thailand	Thai	Thai
Turkey	Turkish	Turkish
Uruguay	Uruguayan	Spanish
Venezuela	Venezuelan	Spanish
Vietnam	Vietnamese	Vietnamese
Yugoslavia	Yugoslavian	Serbo-Croatian, Slovenian, Macedonian

GRAMMAR SUMMARY

Unit 1

This	is	a fish.
	is not isn't	an octopus.

Is	this	a fish?	Yes, it is.	
			No, it	is not. isn't.
What is What's	this?		It is It's	a fish.

Here is Here's	**my** book. **your** book.

Unit 2

Who is Who's	that?
That is That's	Jim.

He is **He's**		Debbie's brother.
He	is not isn't	an artist.
Is he		a student?
Yes, he is.		

What's **his** name?

Who is Who's	that?
That is That's	Debbie.

She is **She's**		Jim's sister.
She	is not isn't	Jim's friend.
Is she		an artist?
No, she isn't.		

What's **her** name?

Unit 3

The octopus is	green.	
It is It's	in under	the box.

What color is	the box?	It is It's	red.
Where is Where's	the octopus?	It is It's	in the box.

Which box?	The red box.

Unit 4

Those girls are	students.
They are **They're**	art students.
They are not They aren't	from Riverdale.

Are they	in Riverdale? at school? from Riverdale?	Yes, they are. No, they aren't.

Where are they from?	They're from Canada.

You are **You're**	a good singer.	
Are you	a good student?	Yes, **I** am. No, **I'm** not.

Unit 5

Look at	**these**	**men.** **women.**

Their names are	Mr. White and Mr. Black. Miss Green and Mrs. Brown.	
They are They're	English. American.	
Are they	sad? happy?	Yes, they are. No, they aren't.

How old are you?
I'm thirteen years **old.**

We are **We're**	students.	
Are you	actors? English?	Yes, **we** are. No, **we** aren't.

Unit 6

Whose car is that?
It's Tony**'s.**

Unit 7

There is **There's**	a museum in Riverdale.
There are	**some** old houses in Riverdale.

Is there	a movie theater?	Yes, there is. No, there isn't.
Are there	**any** churches?	Yes, there are. No, there aren't.

How many lions are there?
There are two.

There are **some**	trees in the park.
There are**n't any**	

Unit 8

Debbie	**can**	sing.	
Jim	**cannot** **can't**	sing.	
Can	Jim Debbie	play the guitar?	Yes, he can. No, she can't.

Unit 9

What can you see in this square?

There is a glass in this picture. Can you see **it?**
There are two faces in this picture. Can you see **them?**

Unit 10

What time is it?	It is It's	two o'clock.

What is What's	he doing?	He is He's	playing the guitar.
What are	they doing?	They are They're	singing.

I	am	at home.	Anita is with	**me.**
He	is			**him.**
She				**her.**
We	are			**us.**
You				**you.**
They				**them.**

What are you doing?
I'm making dinner.

Tim is sitting	in front of behind next to	Mary. Jim. Isabel. John.

Unit 11

These men are	talking.	
They are not They aren't	leaving.	
Are they	fighting?	Yes, they are. No, they aren't.

What is What's	happening?

GRAMMAR INDEX

adj = adjective; irreg = irregular;
pl = plural; pron = pronoun; sing = singular

WORD LIST

The numbers after each word indicate the page number where the word first appears. An asterisk (*) indicates the word is intended for recognition only on that page.

adj = adjective; *adv* = adverb; *aux* = auxiliary verb; *conj* = conjunction; *interj* = interjection; *n* = noun; *prep* = preposition; *pron* = pronoun; *v* = verb

pl = plural; *sing* = singular

We wish to thank the following for providing us with photographs:

Page 5, pic. 1: National Archaeological Museum, Athens; pic. 2: Bodleian Library, Oxford (MS. Arch. Selden A.1, f.54r.); pic. 3: *droit dia* Lauros-Giraudon, Paris; pic. 4: Peter Clayton; pic. 5: detail, Copyright © 1978 By The Metropolitan Museum of Art; pic. 6: detail, Copyright © 1978 By The Metropolitan Museum of Art, Rogers Fund, 1933. **Page 10,** pic. 1: DC Comics Inc.; pic. 2: The Boston Symphony Orchestra; pic. 3: Central Office of Information, London; pic. 4: Black Bull Music, Inc. **Page 11,** pic. 5: From the motion picture "On Golden Pond" (Universal, 1981), Courtesy of Universal Pictures; pic. 6: DC Comics Inc. **Page 22:** Mercedes Lois Ecos de España (Photo Otto Berk). **Page 24,** top: David Thorpe; bottom: Robert Ellis. **Page 26,** © Laurence Whistler. **Page 28,** pics. 1 and 2: Los Angeles Dodgers; pics. 3 and 4: The Cosmos Soccer Club; pics. 5 and 6: Swimming World; pics. 7 and 8: Carol Newsom. **Page 29,** pic. 9: New York Jets; pic. 10: Thomas J. Croke, Team Photographer, New England Patriots. **Page 36:** David Redfern, London. **Page 37:** Peter Lake. **Page 40,** top: Peter Lake; bottom: Tom Leung. **Page 53:** The Philadelphia Museum of Art: The A. E. Gallatin Collection. **Page 55:** © BEELDRECHT, Amsterdam/ VAGA, New York, Collection Haags Gemeentemuseum—The Hague. **Page 65,** pic. 1: Kunsthistorisches Museum, Vienna; pic. 2: Scala, Florence; pic. 3: Collection The Solomon R. Guggenheim Museum, New York—Henri Rousseau, The Football Players, 1908. (Photo Robert E. Mates); pic. 4: The Louvre, Paris.

We wish to thank the following artists:

Cover: Kimmerle Milnazik.

Debbie Dieneman, Robert Jackson, Gloria Jean Moyer, Judy Hans Price, Paul Undersinger and Alan Wallerstein.

Linden Artists: Jon Davis, Graham Allen, Colin Newman, Valerie Sangster, Clive Spong and Brian Watson.

Answers to riddles

Page 49: A man can ride an elephant, but an elephant cannot ride a man.

Page 67: A table.